# 50 State Guide
# Firearm Laws and Regulations

A traveler's resource for the concealed carry laws of all 50 states and the District of Columbia.

**2021 Edition**

## User-Friendly Overviews of essential information like:

- Interstate Transport of Firearms
- Airports
- Canada
- Mexico
- BLM Land
- Castle Doctrine
- National Parks and Monuments
- U.S. Army Corps of Engineers

- Indian Reservations
- Police Encounters
- "No Guns Allowed" Signs
- Buying and Selling Firearms
- Federal Buildings
- NFA Weapon Laws

Copyright © 2021 by Legal Heat

Written and published in the United States of America by Legal Heat

ISBN: 978-0-9966652-2-3

**Legal Heat**
P.O. Box 22694
Cleveland OH 44122
Email: contact@mylegalheat.com
Website: www.LegalHeat.com

# Disclaimer

The information contained in this book is intended as background educational material that may be of assistance to the reader; it is not, however, offered as legal advice and does not take the place of legal counsel. The authors have made attempts to ensure the accuracy and reliability of the information provided in this book. However, federal, state and local statutes, rules and regulations are subject to change and are open to differing interpretations. Therefore, prior to carrying or being in possession of a firearm/weapon, the user of this book must always consult an attorney and/or local law enforcement to confirm the laws of the applicable jurisdiction. The user hereby assumes the full risk associated with the use of this book by the user and reliance upon the information provided in this book. The information in this book is provided "as is" without warranty of any kind. All express and implied warranties related to this book and its content are hereby disclaimed. The authors of this book and National Training Solutions, INC d/b/a Legal Heat and their respective members, managers, employees, agents, independent contractors and attorneys (collectively herein, the "Author Parties") do not accept, and hereby expressly disclaim, any responsibility or liability for the accuracy, content, completeness, legality or reliability of the information contained in this book. The user is advised and agrees that the Author Parties are under no obligation to update the information contained in this book based upon changes in the law or otherwise.

No warranties, promises and/or representations of any kind, expressed or implied, are given as to the nature, standard, accuracy or otherwise of the information provided in this book nor to the suitability or otherwise of the information to your particular circumstances. The Author Parties shall not be liable for, and the user on behalf of himself/herself and his/her heirs, personal representatives, successors and assigns hereby knowingly and voluntarily releases the Author Parties from, any and all costs, expenses, losses, claims, causes of action or damages of whatever nature (direct, indirect, consequential, or other), known or unknown, whether arising in contract, tort or otherwise, which may arise as a result of the user's use of (or inability to use) this book, or from the user's use of (or failure to use) the information contained in this book. If and to the extent this book provides references to websites owned by third parties, the content of such third party sites is not within our control, and we cannot and will not take responsibility for the information or content thereon nor that such sites are free from computer viruses or anything else that has destructive properties.

By using this book and/or viewing the information contained in this book, the user agrees to all of the above terms and conditions and acknowledges the user's understanding of, and voluntary agreement to, the waivers, disclaimers, agreements and releases set forth above.

## About the Author

Phil Nelsen is an attorney, tenure-track college professor, former prosecutor and professional firearm instructor. Phil has the pleasure of routinely speaking at firearm law conferences throughout the United States and is honored to be regularly called on to advise on key firearm law issues by some of the world's largest firearm dealers and manufacturers, as well members of the United States Congress. Together with his brother Jason, Phil founded the nationwide firearms training firm, Legal Heat, in 2006. Legal Heat has since certified in excess of 250,000 students to obtain concealed firearm permits. He is the author of *Legal Heat: 50 State Guide to Firearm Laws* in traditional and app format, available on all major platforms. Phil has been featured in Forbes and is a guest commentator on several national media programs.

Phil lives in the Rocky Mountains (only a few minutes from the late-great John Moses Browning) with his beautiful wife, children, and all the freedom he can find. In his free time Phil works as a professional big game hunting guide, where he has guided over 100 successful hunts throughout the Western United States.

For media or other inquiries Phil can be contacted at contact@mylegalheat.com or www.philnelsen.com.

## About Legal Heat

Legal Heat is one of, if not the, largest civilian firearm training and firearms law publishing firms in America. Since its founding in 2006, Legal Heat has qualified roughly 300,000 people for their concealed carry permits in nearly 200 locations across the country, in large format retail outdoor stores and independent merchants. Legal Heat is the exclusive firearm-training partner for some of the largest firearm retailers in America, and has taught thousands of training courses ranging in duration from 4 hours, to several days.

All Legal Heat instructors are highly experienced experts in the safe and legal use of firearms and have legal, military, law or other professional backgrounds. All Legal Heat instructors are certified by the National Rifle Association and various other state certifying agencies.

If you would like to find or host a training course in your area, or join our team as an instructor, you can visit our website at: www.legalheat.com

# Introduction

This book was born out of necessity. As a young firearm instructor in the early 2000s I find myself traveling the country teaching training courses. One week I would be in Wisconsin, the next Pennsylvania, and the next California. I found myself constantly frustrated by the lack of reliable information related to transporting and possessing firearms in all the various states. The Bureau of Alcohol and Tobacco reports that each year over 1,600,000 handguns are manufactured in the United States, and it is estimated that roughly 1 in 20 adults now have a concealed carry permit. As most gun owners are aware, laws regulating firearms in the United States vary dramatically. What you might get a tip of the hat for doing in Wyoming, will get you five years in a New York state prison.

With so many people carrying firearms throughout the United States, and the devastating consequences that can accompany firearm violations, you might assume it would be easy to find some sort of reference guide to help the average law abiding citizen avoid drastic punishments for inadvertent mistakes. You may think that, but you'd be wrong, until now. Legal Heat, first published in 2008, has sold tens of thousands of copies and has become an invaluable resource for the gun owner community.

This book was written and designed for the sole purpose of providing a quick reference guide to the average traveler who would like to defend him or herself while traveling throughout this great nation. We have compiled the most essential of information from all fifty states and the District of Columbia, and have organized it in a user-friendly format. You will find each state has its own page containing the following information:

- **Constitutional Provision for the Right to Bear Arms:** A great deal can be learned about a state's views on firearms simply by examining their state Constitution.

- **Ratings:** We have rated the state's friendliness towards concealed carry based on our personal experiences, statutes, cases, prohibited areas, and attorney general opinions. The scale goes from 1-5 stars, with five being the most friendly.

- **Contact Information:** Contact information for each state's permit issuing authority.

- **Prohibited areas**: Places where you cannot carry your concealed firearm even if your permit is recognized by the state you are in.

- **Reciprocity:** A list of permits each state recognizes.

- **Special notes:** Any special notes that we feel you should be aware of.

This book is not intended to offer you legal advice or to be a legal treatise on state firearm laws. Such an endeavor would be far more complicated, and would cost substantially more than what you paid for this guide. This book was written and compiled by experienced attorneys and firearm instructors who possess various formal certifications. This is a work of passion, and necessity, to help guide firearm owners to stay on the right side of the law. Near the end of this book you will find the contact information for all of the Attorney General's offices in the United States, please contact the appropriate state authority with any additional questions or concerns.

Finally, we thank you for being a responsible citizen. A citizen who refuses to be a victim that simply bows to the will of the unjust and the evil. It has been said, and we concur, *all that is necessary for the triumph of evil, is that good men (and women) do nothing.*

## How To Stay Up To Date On Law Changes

As is the nature of the legislative process, the laws contained in this book are subject to change throughout the year without notice. Have no fear, however, because we have developed a way to stay up to date on all law changes that might occur during the year. Simply take out your smartphone and scan the below image with your camera. You will be taken to a digital summary of all the laws contained in this book. We recommend always checking the digital version before you travel to make sure nothing has changed. This is a free service included with your purchase of this book.

Throughout this book you will see various other scannable features, similar to the one above. Some will take you to video overviews of legal topics, while others will take you practical tips or discounts.

# Table of Contents

Things to Know ........................................................................................1

**Interstate Transport of Firearms**.........................................................2

Airlines and Airports ..............................................................................5
National Parks and Monuments..............................................................6
Indian Reservations................................................................................6
BLM Land...............................................................................................7
AMTRAK..................................................................................................7
Transport Into Canada ...........................................................................8
Transport Into Mexico.............................................................................9
Current and Retired Police Officers ........................................................9
What to do During a Police Encounter ..................................................11
Posted Buildings ("No Guns" Signs) .....................................................13
What is the Castle Doctrine? ................................................................13
May Issue vs. Shall Issue States..........................................................13
Buying or Selling a Firearm...................................................................14

**Federal Prohibited Areas** ....................................................................17

Post Offices ..........................................................................................18
Federal Facilities ..................................................................................19
Military Bases........................................................................................19
Veteran Affairs Property ........................................................................20
School Zones.........................................................................................20
U.S. Army Corps of Engineers Property ................................................21

**State Summary Pages** .........................................................................23

Alabama................................................................................................24
Alaska ..................................................................................................26
Arizona .................................................................................................28
Arkansas...............................................................................................30
California ...............................................................................................35
Colorado ...............................................................................................37
Connecticut ..........................................................................................39
Delaware...............................................................................................41
Florida ..................................................................................................43
Georgia.................................................................................................45
Hawaii ..................................................................................................48
Idaho ....................................................................................................49
Illinois...................................................................................................51
Indiana .................................................................................................54

Iowa................................................................56
Kansas ..........................................................58
Kentucky .......................................................60
Louisiana ......................................................62
Maine ...........................................................64
Maryland .......................................................66
Massachusetts................................................68
Michigan .......................................................70
Minnesota......................................................73
Mississippi.....................................................75
Missouri ........................................................79
Montana........................................................82
Nebraska.......................................................84
Nevada ..........................................................86
New Hampshire..............................................88
New Jersey .....................................................90
New Mexico....................................................92
New York........................................................94
North Carolina ...............................................96
North Dakota .................................................99
Ohio.............................................................102
Oklahoma .....................................................104
Oregon .........................................................107
Pennsylvania .................................................110
Rhode Island.................................................112
South Carolina...............................................113
South Dakota.................................................116
Tennessee .....................................................118
Texas............................................................120
Utah.............................................................123
Vermont ........................................................125
Virginia.........................................................127
Washington....................................................129
Washington D.C..............................................131
West Virginia .................................................134
Wisconsin .....................................................136
Wyoming.......................................................138

**Draw Your Own Reciprocity Map**..................................**140**

**State Attorney General Contact Information** .....................**141**

**50 State NFA Weapon Law Summaries** ...........................**143**

**Duty To Retreat Law Summaries** ....................................................**149**

**Second Amendment Articles Written By The Author** ........................**157**

Article 1: The Constitution Does Not Care How Much Harm Guns Cause... And That Is A Good Thing. ..........................................................................157
Article 2: A Pragmatic Argument In Favor Of Letting Teachers Be Armed..........162
Article 3: On Interacting With Law Enforcement..................................168

**STAY LEGAL. STAY SAFE.**..........................................................**172**

Notes ...................................................................................175
Notes ...................................................................................176
Notes ...................................................................................177

# Things to Know

Key Law Summaries for:

- Interstate Vehicle Transport of Firearms
- Airlines and Airports
- National Parks and Monuments
- Tribal Land
- BLM Land
- AMTRAK
- Canada Transport
- Mexico Transport
- Law Enforcement Officers Safety Act (LEOSA)
- What to do During a Police Encounter
- Posted Buildings ("No Gun" Signs)
- Castle Doctrine
- May Issue vs. Shall Issue
- Buying or Selling Firearms
- Federal Prohibited Areas

# Interstate Transport of Firearms

## Vehicle Transport

**How to transport a firearm from state to state in your vehicle (*McClure –Volkmer Rule*)**

In response to reports of hunters and other gun owners being arrested while transporting their firearms through states with tight gun control, Congress passed Senate Bill 2414 as part of the 1986 Firearm Owners Protection Act ("FOPA"). This law, called the *McClure-Volkmer Rule*, provides protection for gun owners transporting firearms through restrictive states, subject to strict requirements.

**Federal Statute (*McClure-Volkmer Rule*):** Notwithstanding any other provision of any law or any rule or regulation of a State or any political subdivision thereof, any person who is not otherwise prohibited by this chapter from transporting, shipping, or receiving a firearm shall be entitled to transport a firearm for any lawful purpose from any place where he may lawfully possess and carry such firearm to any other place where he may lawfully possess and carry such firearm if, during such transportation the firearm is unloaded, and neither the firearm nor any ammunition being transported is readily accessible or is directly accessible from the passenger compartment of such transporting vehicle: Provided, That in the case of a vehicle without a compartment separate from the driver's compartment the firearm or ammunition shall be contained in a locked container other than the glove compartment or console. (18 U.S.C. 926A, 27 CFR 178.38.)

**Plain Talk Explanation:** Some states will either recognize your concealed firearm permit, or will simply allow you to carry a loaded firearm while in their state, but some states will do neither. When traveling through restricted states (i.e. states that do not honor your concealed firearm permit) you can still have your firearm in your vehicle, but you need to abide by specific rules.

In order to ensure compliance with the above federal law you must abide by the following 5 steps:

1.  You must be traveling:

    a.  FROM a place where you may lawfully possess and/or carry the firearm (such as your home state);

    b.  TO any other place where you may lawfully possess and/or carry that same firearm (such as a state that honors your permit and allows the type of weapon being transported).

2.  The firearm(s) must be unloaded.

3.  The firearm(s) and ammunition must be stored separately (i.e. separate containers).

4.  The firearm(s) and ammunition must be stored so they are not readily or directly accessible from the passenger compartment of the vehicle. (i.e. must be in the trunk of your vehicle if possible). If you have a trunk, you must store your weapons in the trunk.

a. If your vehicle does not have a trunk, the completely unloaded firearm must be LOCKED in a hard sided case. The glove box or center console does NOT satisfy this requirement. The firearm MUST be stored in a separate locked case. Put the case as far away from you, in the driver seat, as possible.

5. In order to guarantee federal protection, your transport through the state should be continuous and uninterrupted. This means you are not a tourist at any time. As a general rule you should not spend more than 24 hours inside the jurisdiction

Whenever you are transporting a firearm through a state that prohibits your right to carry it is <u>highly</u> recommended that you <u>always</u> store your firearm in a locked (hard-sided) container than the ammunition. If your vehicle has a trunk, both the firearm(s) and the ammunition must be stored in the trunk. If your vehicle does not have a trunk, then your firearms must be in a locked hard-sided container and both the firearms and ammunition must be stored as far from you in the drivers seat as possible.

Once the above 5 steps have been satisfied you are entitled, under federal law, to lawfully transport a firearm in your vehicle. Some states do not require you to complete all of the above steps, but some do. New York, New Jersey and California, for example, are responsible for nearly every case on the books dealing with this law. Because of the extreme penalties that can accompany inadvertent mistakes, always follow these five steps to avoid any confusion and ensure complete compliance to the law.

If you are visiting a restricted state for a prolonged period of time, such as a vacation, the federal law discussed in this section will not offer you protection. You will need to verify what is required by the state where you will be visiting <u>before</u> transporting your firearm to that state.

**What About Transporting High Capacity Magazines, "Assault Weapons" or Other Prohibited Items Through A State?**

It is important to understand that, although this federal law allows you to transport some firearms through restrictive states, it does not allow you to transport items that are prohibited under state law, such as high capacity magazines or "assault weapons".

In one of the few cases that addressed this specific question, the court ruled that the federal law discussed above (18 U.S.C.A. § 926A) **does not prohibit states from enforcing bans on large capacity magazines or bans on other weapons (like "assault firearms")**. Meaning, if the item you are transporting is prohibited in the state through which you plan on transporting it, the federal law discussed in this lesson will not protect you and you will still be charged with a crime. As such, it is essential that you know the laws of the states through which you will be transporting your firearms. (see Coal. of New Jersey Sportsmen v. Florio, 744 F. Supp. 602 (D.N.J. 1990)).

**How Long Can I Be In A State And Still Be Considered "Transporting"?**

Great question. There is no solid answer to this question as the law does not provide a time threshold and there are very few court cases dealing with this question.

In one of the only cases dealing with this specific question, a man named Paul Guisti was arrested for having an unloaded .45–caliber pistol in a locked safe inside of his boat which he was navigating in the waters just off shore from New York. Paul had skippered his boat from his home in Florida, along the eastern seaboard to New York, and then planned on returning to Florida prior to being arrested. Given that Paul was acting as more of a tourist than a transporter in New York, the federal law discussed above does not protect him from prosecution. In this case, the defendant was not transporting his gun interstate, but rather, admits he was traveling along the Eastern seaboard, docking in various states for undefined periods of time. This is more of a tourist activity. The court reasoned as follows:

"The Court is not persuaded that the [18 USC § 926A] applies to interstate travel which is in actuality a round-trip foray with a gun into states that the defendant is not entitled to possess the gun. The plain language of the statute mandates application only if the defendant was transporting the gun from one state to a different state." (See People v. Guisti, 30 Misc. 3d 1229(A), 926 N.Y.S.2d 345 (Crim. Ct. 2011)).

Although it doesn't provide a clear answer of what timeframe would be considered transporting, it is clear the courts will look into the facts of each case to determine if you are a tourist or a transporter. In other words, if you plan on visiting Disneyland, staying multiple days to see the sights, or doing other tourist related activities, you should not plan on having the protection of this federal law.

## What About Other Vehicles Without Trunks, Like Single-Cab Pickups or Motorcycles?

There are virtually no court cases addressing specific vehicle types. Congress did include an exception for vehicles lacking a trunk – such as pickup trucks or motorcycles. For these, the firearm must "be contained in a locked container other than the glove compartment or console." While debating how exactly someone should transport the firearm on their motorcycle the Senate said:

"It is anticipated that the firearms being transported will be made inaccessible in a way consistent with the mode of transportation–in a trunk in vehicles which have such containers, or in a case or similar receptacle in vehicles which do not." (See S. Rep. No. 476, 97th Cong., 2d Sess. 25 (1982))

Legal Heat's advice is to make the firearm as inaccessible as possible to you in the driver's (rider's) position, ensuring that the firearm you are transporting is locked inside a hard-sided container and the ammunition is stored separately from the firearm. Source: 8 U.S.C. 926A, 27 CFR 178.38.

# Airlines and Airports

**Transporting Firearms:** A passenger on an aircraft may transport a firearm in his or her checked baggage, so long as all TSA regulations are followed. Always abide by the following steps when traveling with a firearm, and check with your particular airline about any other procedures they may have:

1. All firearms must be declared to the air carrier during the ticket counter check-in process.

2. The firearm must be unloaded.

3. The firearm must be carried in a hard-sided container.

4. The container must be locked. Make certain the container is locked in a way that it cannot be pried open on either side. Use multiple locks if necessary.

5. The passenger must provide the key to the screener if it is necessary to open the container, and then remain present during screening to take back possession of the key after the container is cleared.

6. Any ammunition transported must be securely packed in fiber (such as cardboard), wood or metal boxes or other packaging specifically designed to carry small amounts of ammunition.

7. Firearm magazines/clips do not satisfy the packaging requirement unless they provide a complete and secure enclosure of the ammunition (e.g., by securely covering the exposed portions of the magazine or by securely placing the magazine in a pouch, holder, holster or lanyard).

8. The ammunition may also be located in the same hard-sided case as the firearm, as long as it is properly packed as described above.

9. Black powder and percussion caps used with black-powder type firearms are not permitted in carry-on or checked baggage

10. Airlines may have their own additional requirements on the carriage of firearms and the amount of ammunition that you may have in your checked baggage. Therefore, travelers should also contact the airline regarding its firearm and ammunition carriage policies.

**Transporting Ammunition:** Ammunition is prohibited in carry-on baggage, but may be transported in checked baggage. Firearm magazines and ammunition clips, whether loaded or empty, must be securely boxed or included within a hard-sided case containing an unloaded firearm.

Small arms ammunition, including ammunition not exceeding .75 caliber and shotgun shells of any gauge, may be carried in the same hard-sided case as the firearm.

Law Source: Title 49: Transportation - Part 1540- Civil Aviation Security - §1540.111 Carriage of weapons, explosives, and incendiaries by individuals.

# National Parks and Monuments

For 27 years in the United States there existed a federal ban on firearms in, or on the grounds of, any national park or monument. The ban was set in place by the Reagan administration and was designed to reduce violent crime, and deter negative environmental impacts caused by firearms in National Parks. The ban explicitly prohibited the carry or possession of any firearm into any national park or monument. On 05/22/09 President Obama signed a bill *(Credit Card Accountability Responsibility and Disclosure (CARD) Act, H.R. 627, or §512(b))* that overturned the 27-year prohibition. The law now allows anyone to carry a firearm into any of the 392 locations under the control of the National Parks Service **so long as the state they are located in would otherwise recognize their right to carry a firearm** (either through permit reciprocity or state law).

Further, §512(b) states: The Secretary of the Interior shall not promulgate or enforce any regulation that prohibits an individual from possessing a firearm including an assembled or functional firearm in any unit of the National Park System or the National Wildlife Refuge System if—

(1)  The individual is not otherwise prohibited by law from possessing the firearm; and

(2)  The possession of the firearm is in compliance with the law of the State in which the unit of the National Park System or the National Wildlife Refuge System is located.

In other words, there is no longer a difference between the national park/ monument located within a particular state, and the rest of the state, unless the state has explicitly stated so. Note, however, that even if you are allowed to carry into a particular national park or monument, you still will not be able to carry into any of the occupied buildings within the park as these are considered "federal buildings" (see Federal Entities below). **The law took effect February 22nd 2010. Permission to carry a firearm into a park and the actual restrictions on such possession will vary by state. The federal law is governed by each state's firearm laws. Check with the individual state and park regarding its laws and prohibition before arrival.**

# Indian Reservations

Each Indian Nation operates as a limited sovereign nation under the observation of the United States Department of the Interior's Bureau of Indian Affairs division. As a result of this limited sovereignty each Nation is given discretion over certain laws and regulations, including firearm laws. Although the Tribes work closely with the Federal government, the tribal council, not the local or Federal government, has jurisdiction over the reservation. There are currently 310 Indian Tribes in the United States, each possessing their own laws regarding the transportation, carry, and possession of firearms. Unfortunately many of these laws are unpublished. Prior to entering a reservation, contact the tribal counsel to assure compliance with the law.

# BLM Land

As a general rule, if you are allowed to legally carry a firearm, either by permit reciprocity or local law, in the state that the BLM land is found then carry onto the BLM property should also be allowed. If the area is restricted, it will more than likely be posted as a prohibited area by state or federal law. State and local laws relating to the use of firearms or other weapons apply on public lands due to proximity to residential areas, high recreational use, or other resource concerns. Buildings found on BLM property, however, are usually Federal buildings and would thus be off limits to firearms per Federal law (see the "Federal Prohibited Areas" section for an overview of what buildings are off limits). Contact the governing entity with any questions regarding BLM property to ensure compliance to the law.

# AMTRAK

AMTRAK is a government owned rail-corporation designed for passenger commuting throughout the United States. Being owned and operated by a government entity (The National Railroad Passenger Corporation) AMTRAK generally has the right to determine its own rules regarding the possession of firearms on its trains and property. However, recent Congressional action has expanded the right of passengers to transport firearms while traveling on AMTRAK. On December 16, 2009, the President signed the Consolidated Appropriations Act, 2010 (Public Law 111-117) into law. Section 159 of the legislation directs the National Railroad Passenger Corporation (AMTRAK) to develop the ability to transport firearms in checked baggage, similar to the program used by the airlines. The current process is as follows:

1. At the station of departure, the passenger can only obtain their ticket from an AMTRAK ticket agent at the ticket counter (kiosk or automated processing is not permitted). When the AMTRAK ticket agent accesses the passengers reservation record, there will be a notification the passenger has indicated they will be transporting a firearm in checked baggage.

2. The AMTRAK ticket agent will issue the passenger a firearms checked baggage ticket and will also be responsible for issuing a Firearms Declaration form for each checked firearm. A ticket will be generated for each firearm to provide a confirmation tool for baggage agents that reservations and space exists on the train that the passenger is checking the firearm.

3. The passenger will complete the Declaration form and return it to the AMTRAK agent

4. The AMTRAK agent will separate the two part Declaration form, retaining one copy for AMTRAK records

5. The baggage agent (or ticket agent where they perform both functions) will lift the ticket and place a baggage tag on the suitcase for handguns. The ticket for the firearm, the station copies of the Firearms Declaration form, and baggage tag will be maintained at the station of origin

6. The agent will then ask the passenger to open their baggage containing the firearm and place a hard copy of the declaration form inside the baggage and visually verify that the firearm is in an acceptable hard-sided, locked container

a. If the container is not hard-sided, locked, or acceptable the AMTRAK agent will deny transportation to the passenger until such time as the firearm is compliant with AMTRAK movement requirements.

7. Once the passenger has secured their baggage, the AMTRAK agent will take charge of the baggage and it will be moved through the normal AMTRAK checked baggage process. When checked baggage (with a handgun inside) arrives at the destination, the process is reversed.

8. Checked baggage is unloaded from the train baggage car/area by the conductor or employee assigned and transported by the AMTRAK agent to the passenger baggage retrieval area or baggage carousel.

9. AMTRAK agents will follow standard procedures to verify passenger baggage claim check stubs with the applicable baggage destination tag(s).

AMTRAK does not permit passengers to transport black powder or percussion caps used in connection with black powder firearms in their checked or carry-on baggage.

# Transport Into Canada

Canada has very strict laws governing transportation of handguns and "military type" long guns. United States citizens may, however, bring "sporting" rifles and shotguns into Canada. These must be declared to Customs officials when entering Canada. Certain handguns and other non-restricted weapons may be brought into Canada if a permit to transport has first has been obtained from Canadian authorities. There are three classes of firearms in Canada:

**Non-restricted** (most common rifles and shotguns): These may generally be imported for purposes such as hunting, protection from wild animals in remote wilderness areas where firearms are allowed, or target-shooting. They may also be taken in transit through Canada by a reasonably direct route.

**Restricted:** (longer-barreled handguns, some types of long guns) These are allowed for certain purposes, such as target shooting at an approved club or range, but they are not allowed for hunting or self protection.

**Prohibited:** (shorter-barreled handguns, automatic weapons) These cannot be brought into Canada.

**Prior to departing for Canada be sure to comply with the following steps:**

1. Declare firearms in writing, in triplicate, using the Non-Resident Firearm Declaration (form CAFC 909).

2. If there are more than three firearms, a Non-Resident Firearm Declaration Continuation Sheet (form CAFC 910) should be added.

3. The declaration form should be filled out prior to arrival at the point of entry, in order to save time. However, it should not be signed before arriving at the entry point, as a Canada Border Services Agency (CBSA) customs officer must witness the signature.

4. Once the declaration has been confirmed by the CBSA customs officer, it acts as a license for the owner and as a temporary registration certificate for the firearms brought to Canada; and it is valid for 60 days. The declaration can be renewed for free, providing it is renewed before it expires, by contacting the Chief Firearms Officer (CFO) (call 1-800-731-4000) of the relevant province or territory.

5. A confirmed declaration costs a flat fee of $25, regardless of the number of firearms listed on it. It is valid only for the person who signs it and only for those firearms listed on the declaration. (see: http://www.rcmp-grc.gc.ca/cfp-pcaf/fs-fd/restr-eng.htm).

## Transport Into Mexico

**MEXICO:** Mexico allows for the transport of 2 sporting rifles or shotguns of an acceptable caliber and/or 50 rounds of ammunition for hunting purposes. You must obtain the following documentation and abide by the following steps prior to departing for Mexico:

1. A tourist permit must be obtained from the Mexican Consulate having jurisdiction over the area where the visitor resides.

2. If the permit is obtained, Mexican immigration officials will place a firearms stamp on this permit at the point of entry.

3. A certificate of good conduct issued by the prospective hunter's local police department,

4. Proof of citizenship,

5. A passport and five passport size photos,

6. A hunting services agreement with the Mexican Secretary of Urban Development and Ecology (issued by a Mexican Forestry and Wildlife Office),

7. A military permit (issued by the Military Post and valid for only 90 days)

All these documents must be in the hunter's possession.

All firearms must be declared and registered with United States Customs on Form 4457 or any other registration document available for the purpose of facilitating reentry into the United States with the same firearms.

## Current and Retired Police Officers

Exemption of qualified law enforcement officers from state laws prohibiting the carrying of concealed firearms.

The Law Enforcement Officers Safety Act of 2004 (Ch. 44 T 18, USC §926B and §926C) allows an active or "Qualified Retired Law Enforcement Officer" to carry a concealed firearm in all US states (T. 18 § 921 includes the District of Columbia, Puerto Rico, and other U.S. Possessions as "States"). Active officers must be in good standing, and have proper photo identification. Retired officers must have held a law enforcement position for 10 years, separated in good standing, and meet agency standards for active duty officers each year. A more detailed summary is below. We recommend contacting your local police department for more details on qualification under LEOSA.

## Active Officers

1. Qualified law enforcement officers with proper identification may carry a concealed firearm regardless of any State law, or laws enacted by its political subdivisions. However, restrictions still apply to private property and buildings, parks, installations, and government property covered by State law.
   a. Proper Identification is photographic identification that shows the individual is a police officer or law enforcement officer of an agency.
   b. Qualified officers are
      i. authorized by their agency to carry a firearm,
      ii. have police powers,
      iii. are not subject to discipline that could revoke or suspend police powers,
      iv. are not under the influence of alcohol or another intoxicating substance,
      v. are not prohibited under federal law from receiving a firearm.
2. Qualified law enforcement officers cannot carry ammunition prohibited by federal law, machine guns, silencers, or any destructive devices.

## Retired Officers

1. Qualified retired law enforcement officers with proper identification may carry a concealed firearm regardless of any State law, or laws enacted by its political subdivisions. However, restrictions still apply to private property and buildings, parks, installations, and government property covered by State law.
   a. Proper Identification is photographic identification that shows the individual was a police officer or law enforcement officer of an agency and has been qualified within the past year as meeting the qualifications for active duty to carry a firearm. See 18 U.S.C. § 926C(d).
   b. Qualified retired officers:
      i. Separated in good standing as a law enforcement officer (also included are AMTRAK police, Federal Reserve Police, and LEO of the Executive branch), other than for reasons of mental instability. See 18 U.S.C. § 926C(c)(1);
      ii. Had police powers. See 18 U.S.C. § 926C(c)(3)(A-B);
      iii. Served as a law enforcement officer for a combined 10 years. See 18 U.S.C. § 926C(c)(3)(A-B);
      iv. Completed any probationary period of service due to disability;
      v. During the last 12 months and at their own expense, met the standards for qualification in firearm training for active officers;
      vi. Are not prohibited due to mental health as determined by a physician employed by the agency;
      vii. Are not under the influence of alcohol. See 18 U.S.C. § 926C(c)(6);

viii. Are not prohibited under federal law from receiving a firearm;

ix. The firearm that you intend to carry pursuant to § 926C is properly registered to you pursuant to any applicable state or municipal laws; and,

x. The firearm that you are carrying concealed is not one of the following: machine gun (as defined in § 5845 of the National Firearm Act); silencer (as defined in § 921 of Chapter 44 of the Title 18, United States Code); destructive device (as defined in § 921 of Chapter 44 of the Title 18, United States Code). See 18 U.S.C. § 926C(e)(1-3).

## What to do During a Police Encounter

Scan Here

Some states impose a statutory duty upon permit holders that legally requires them to inform a police officer of the presence of a firearm whenever they have an official encounter with an officer. These states are called *"Duty to Inform"* states.

**Duty To Inform States:**

In these states you are required by law to immediately, and affirmatively, tell a police officer if you have a firearm in your possession. If a state has a duty to inform law it will be noted under the special notes section of each state summary page. However, in keeping with our quick reference theme, they are:

- Alaska (Alaska Stat. Ann. §11.61.220)
- Arkansas (Ark Admin. Code 130.00.8-3-2(b))
- Maine: (Permit holders have a quasi duty, non permit holders have full duty to inform).
- Michigan (MCL 28.425f(3))
- Nebraska (Neb. Rev. Stat. §69-2440)
- North Carolina (N.C. Gen. Stat. Ann. §14-415.11)
- Ohio (Ohio Rev. Code Ann. §2923.16)
- Oklahoma (Okla. Stat. Ann. Tit. 21, §1290.8)
- South Carolina (§23-31-215)
- Texas (must provide permit when asked for ID, §411.205)
- Washington D.C. (Title 7 Subtitle J Chpt. 25 § 7-2509.04)

If you find yourself in one of the *Duty to Inform* states you **must** inform an officer if you have a firearm. When informing an officer of a firearm we recommend following these five steps:

1. Keep your hands visible at all times. If you are in a vehicle place your hands on the steering wheel until you have informed the officer of the presence of the firearm, and fully complied with his or her instructions.

2. Advise the officer that you have a valid concealed firearm permit and there is a firearm in your vehicle/possession.

3. Advise the officer of the location of the firearm.

4. Comply fully with all instructions given by the officer.

5. Do not reach for your weapon or permit, or do anything that might be interpreted as reaching for your weapon, unless instructed to do so.

**Quasi Duty To Inform States**:

In addition to the above *Duty to Inform* states, some states have **quasi duty to inform laws**. These laws require that a permit holder must have his/her permit in their possession and <u>surrender it upon the request of an officer</u>. The specific requirements of these laws will vary from state to state, and if a state has a quasi duty to inform law it will be noted under the special notes section of each state summary page. It is important to note that being required to give an officer your permit once it is asked of you (*quasi duty to inform*), and being required to affirmatively tell an officer you have a firearm without being prompted (*duty to inform*) are two very different legal requirements.

**No Duty To Inform States:**

Finally, some states are **No Duty To Inform** states. Meaning, there are no laws that require you to affirmatively inform an officer if you have a firearm, and there are also no laws that require you to respond if asked. In these states the question arises as to whether one should inform an officer about the firearm or not. Our advice is...maybe.

**FULL DISCLOSURE:** A potential outcome of informing an officer that you have a firearm in the vehicle (when not required to do so by state law) is that the officer might then have the ability to perform what is called a *Terry Stop* or a *Terry Frisk*. The *Terry Doctrine* stems from a 1968 Supreme Court case, *Terry v. Ohio*. In *Terry*, the United States Supreme Court held that an officer may perform a protective frisk pursuant to a lawful stop when the officer reasonably believes a person is **"armed and presently dangerous to the officer or others."** (see: 392 U.S. 1, 24, 88 S.Ct. 1868, 20 L.Ed.2d 889 (1968)). The Court further cautioned that a search "is a serious intrusion upon the sanctity of the person" and should not be taken lightly. Id. at 17. The officer must first have a valid reason for stopping the person, and the officer's subsequent actions must be "reasonably related in scope to the circumstances" justifying the stop. The sole purpose for allowing the frisk is to protect the officer and other prospective victims by neutralizing potential weapons. (see: *Michigan v. Long*, 463 U.S. 1032, 1049 n. 14, 103 S.Ct. 3469). Although it is unlikely to occur to a permit holder, a Terry Stop allows a police officer to remove you from your vehicle, pat down all occupants of the vehicle (using the sense of touch to determine if they are armed), as well as search the entire passenger compartment of the vehicle including any locked containers that might reasonably house a weapon.

Legal Heat instructors travel through all 50 states each year and have had many police encounters. We have never had a negative encounter with law enforcement. However, as a criminal defense attorney I also know that relatively nothing good can happen from disclosing information to law enforcement that is not legally required. Our advice is to be aware of your rights and (when not in a *duty to inform* state) use your discretion on whether you want to disclose your firearm or not.

# Posted Buildings ("No Guns" Signs)

As a general rule, private property owners (homeowners or business owners) may apply whatever restrictions they want to their property. Whether these restrictions violate one's individual rights is for the civil courts to decide. A minority of states have gone a step further than the general rule and given business owners legal authority to prohibit firearms on their premises by the posting of "No Guns" signs (see Texas & Wisconsin for example).

A vast majority of states, however, are silent as to whether the posting of a sign has any legal authority to prevent you from carrying your firearm into a business that is open to the public. Whenever a law is ambiguous you should err on the side of caution (so as to not be the test case). We recommend you not carry your firearm into any establishment (private or public) that posts a sign prohibiting firearms. We also recommend you do not patronize such a business.

The most likely penalty a permit holder risks by disobeying a posted sign is the crime of criminal trespass (a simple misdemeanor in most jurisdictions). Generally, with regards to businesses open to the public, one must be affirmatively asked to leave by someone with apparent authority to act on behalf of the owner of the property prior to being charged with criminal trespass. However, as noted above, there are a number of states where merely carrying the firearm into a posted building would result in criminal charges. Understand that your decision to carry a gun into a posted building may or may not carry legal ramifications.

# What is the Castle Doctrine?

The *Castle Doctrine* is a legal doctrine that designates one's place of residence (or, in some states, any place legally occupied, such as one's car, travel trailer, tent, place of work, etc) as a place in which one enjoys protection from illegal trespassing and violent attack. The doctrine gives a person the legal right to use deadly force to defend that place (his/her "castle"), and/or any third party found therein, from violent attack or an illegal entrance, which may lead to violent attack. In a legal context, therefore, castle doctrine mitigates what would otherwise be homicide down to justifiable homicide, which is not criminally punishable.

Many states have instituted castle doctrine laws, with varying degrees of formality. Some doctrines include a legal presumption about when a person would be justified in using deadly force against an intruder, while other states simply state that there is no duty to retreat while inside your home. It is important to note that many states use the term habitation instead of home. Often the term habitation will include hotel rooms, tents, campers, or any dwelling where you will be legally sleeping that night, or have slept the night before. It is important to become informed on each state's castle doctrines as they often dictate the reasonableness of force in defense of habitations, property, and real property. As of 2010 24 states have adopted formal castle doctrines.

# May Issue vs. Shall Issue States

**Shall Issue:** A shall issue state is one that, although it requires a permit in order to carry a concealed firearm, has determined that these permits shall be issued to any applicant that meets basic requirements without any discretion from the issuing authority. Shall issue states are usually required by law to issue a permit to any eligible applicant without proof of reasonable necessity.

**May Issue:** A state that classifies itself as may issue has essentially reserved the right to deny or issue any application, regardless of eligibility, without providing an explanation or appeal. Many of these states do have laws in place to facilitate the issuing of permits, but many, like New York and Hawaii, are notorious for their lack of desire to cooperate.

**Shall Issue States:** Alabama, Alaska, Arizona, Arkansas, Colorado, Florida, Georgia, Idaho, Illinois, Indiana, Iowa, Kansas, Kentucky, Louisiana, Maine, Michigan, Minnesota, Mississippi, Missouri, Montana, Nebraska, Nevada, New Hampshire, New Mexico, North Carolina, North Dakota, Ohio, Oklahoma, Oregon, Pennsylvania, Rhode Island, South Carolina, South Dakota, Tennessee, Texas, Utah, Vermont*, Virginia, Washington, Washington D.C., West Virginia, Wisconsin, Wyoming

**May Issue States:** California, Connecticut, Delaware, Hawaii, Maryland, Massachusetts, New Jersey, New York

## Buying or Selling a Firearm

The laws regarding the private party purchase/sale of handguns vary greatly by state, but there are some general rules you need to be aware of. Private sales (ie. firearms sold by persons other than federally licensed firearm dealers or FFLs) are legal in every state, although some are more regulated than others.

### TO WHOM MAY YOU SELL / GIVE A GUN?

Under federal law (specifically the Gun Control Act of 1968) a person may sell a firearm to an unlicensed resident of his State, if he does not know or have reasonable cause to believe the person is prohibited from receiving or possessing firearms under Federal law. A person may loan or rent a firearm to a resident of any State for temporary use for lawful sporting purposes, if he does not know or have reasonable cause to believe the person is prohibited from receiving or possessing firearms under Federal law. A person may only sell or transfer a firearm to another person if they both reside in the same state.

Likewise a person may only acquire a firearm within the person's own State, except that he or she may purchase or otherwise acquire a rifle or shotgun, in person, at a FFL's premises in any State, provided the sale complies with State laws applicable in the State of sale and the State where the purchaser resides. A person may borrow or rent a firearm in any State for temporary use for lawful sporting purposes.

Source: 18 U.S.C. 922(a)(3) and (5), 922(b)(3), 27 CFR 478.29 and 478.30

## FEDERAL LAW (18 U.S.C. §921, §922, §923)

Under the Gun Control Act of 1968 any person who is "engaged in the business" of selling firearms must be licensed as a federally licensed gun dealer (FFL). One is "engaged in the business" of selling firearms if they, "devotes time, attention, and labor to dealing in firearms as a regular course of trade or business with the principal objective of livelihood and profit through the repetitive purchase and resale of firearms." FFLs have several duties they must fulfill prior to selling a firearm, including performing a background check and maintaining meticulous records of all sales.

Excluded from the federal requirements (and thus the federal record keeping/ background checks) are private parties who, ""make occasional sales, exchanges, or purchases of firearms for the enhancement of a personal collection or for a hobby, or who sells all or part of his personal collection of firearms."

Thus, under federal law a private party is not required to perform a background check, inspect a purchaser's identification, or keep a record of the sale of a firearm. However, state laws may impose such a duty.

## STATE LAWS

Some states impose the same extensive background check duties on private parties as federal law imposes on federal dealers. For example, some states that require the transfer be done through a commercial dealer (i.e. no private party transfers of handguns) include:

- California (Cal. Penal Code § 12072(d))
- Colorado
- Connecticut (Conn. Gen. Stat. § 29)
- Maryland (Md. Code Ann. § 5-101)
- Pennsylvania (18 Pa. Cons. Stat. § 6111)
- Rhode Island (R.I. Gen. Laws § 11-47-35)
- Washington D.C.

Other states have less burdensome procedures, but still require some sort of record keeping, background check, or reporting. This can vary from a simple record (bill of sale) kept in your possession, or a report that must be filed with law enforcement within a certain time period. To complicate factors further, several municipalities have imposed their own record keeping requirements in addition to what the state and federal laws already require. Some of the cities currently requiring additional procedures include:

- Chicago
- New York City
- Omaha
- Columbus

It is crucial that you verify with your state and local law enforcement what procedures may be required prior to selling or purchasing a handgun from a private party.

# Federal Prohibited Areas

Where you can't carry a firearm <u>in any state</u> under federal law

When carrying a firearm in any state there are at least two sets of laws you need to be aware of, state and federal. Each state will have its own laws regarding where you can, and cannot, carry a firearm. These laws are summarized on a state-by-state basis in the next section ("State Summary Pages").

However, regardless of the state you are in, federal law always applies. There are certain areas where firearms are prohibited under federal law, in every state, and most of those areas are summarized below.

1. **Airport Secure Areas (49 CFR § 1540.111(a))**
2. **Post Office Property (18 USC § 930; 39 CFR § 232.1)**
3. **Federal Facilities (18 USC § 930; 36 CFR § 327.13)**
4. **Military Bases (Army Reg. 190-14(2-6);18 USC § 930)**
5. **Veteran Affairs Property (38 C.F.R. § 1.218(a)(13))**
6. **K-12 Schools: Within 1,000 feet of a Public, Parochial or Private K-12 School (18 U.S.C.A. § 922(q)(2)(A))**
    a. **Exceptions apply, see "School Zones" section below.**
7. **Certain Other Federal Property:**
    a. **US Army Corp of Engineers Property (36 C.F.R. § 327.13)**
    b. **The Pentagon Reservation (32 C.F.R. § 234.10)**
    c. **Government Accountability Office Grounds (4 C.F.R. § 25.14)**
    d. **CIA Agency Installation Property (32 C.F.R. § 1903.10)**
    e. **Certain FEMA Property (44 C.F.R. § 15.15)**
    f. **National Military Cemeteries (32 C.F.R. § 553.33)**

Many of these Federal Prohibited Areas have special rules regarding possession of firearms, such as storage in parking lots or certain exceptions for concealed permit holders. A summary of each major prohibited area is provided on the following pages.

# Post Offices

A post office is a federal facility, and is thus the post office building is off limits to firearms in accordance with 18 U.S.C.A. § 930. However, **not only is the post office building off limits to firearms, but the entire property is off limits, including vehicles in the parking lot.**

> *"No person while on postal property may carry firearms, other dangerous or deadly weapons, or explosives, either openly or concealed, or store the same on postal property."*
>
> (see 39 C.F.R. § 232.1(l)).

Possession of Firearms and Other Dangerous Weapons on Postal Property is Prohibited by Law

18 U.S.C. Section 930.
Possession of Firearms and Dangerous Weapons in Federal Facilities

39 CFR 232.1(l).
Weapons and Explosives

Report all firearms violations immediately to the Postal Inspection Service

This prohibition applies to any portions of real property, owned or leased by the Postal Service, that are leased or subleased by the Postal Service to private tenants for their exclusive use.

The general rule with regards to all federal buildings is that you must watch for signs prohibiting firearms posted at the entrance. If you see such a sign, the building is off limits to firearms. With regards to Post Offices, however, the entire property is off limits, including parking lots.

**LEGAL UPDATE FOR POST OFFICES:** Many people are confused about a recent lawsuit out of Colorado regarding firearms in parking lots of Post Offices. Many, including the media, mistakenly believe the case *(Bonidy v. U.S. Postal Serv.)* made it so anyone could now carry a firearm in a post office parking lot. **This is not true** and the prohibition against possessing a firearm on Post Office property still stands. The *Bonidy* case was a District Court case which only applied to that single plaintiff (Tab Bonidy) and which has subsequently been overturned by the Court of Appeals (see Bonidy v. U.S. Postal Serv., No. 13-1374, 2015 WL 3916547 (10th Cir. June 26, 2015).

## Federal Facilities

As a general rule, any federally owned or leased "facility" is off limits to firearms, regardless of what state or province you may be in. The term "Federal facility" means a **building or part thereof owned or leased by the Federal Government, where Federal employees are regularly present for the purpose of performing their official duties.**

These facilities must be posted as off limits to firearms conspicuously, at each public entrance, and no person shall be convicted of an offense if such notice is not so posted at such facility, unless such person had actual notice that the facility prohibited firearms. Actual notice could be a verbal or written communication given to you that firearms were prohibited on the property. (see 18 U.S.C.A. § 930)

**WEAPONS PROHIBITED**

Federal law prohibits the knowing possession or causing to be present of firearms or other dangerous weapons in Federal facilities by all persons not specifically authorized by Title 18 of the United States Code, Section 930 (d). Violators shall be subject to a fine and/or imprisonment in accordance with Section 930 (a) and (b).

## Military Bases

Generally speaking the carrying of firearms onto military installations is against federal law. However, a November 18, 2016 directive, approved by Deputy Secretary of Defense Robert Work, says base commanders, O-5 and above, *"may grant permission to DoD personnel requesting to carry a privately owned firearm (concealed or open carry) on DoD property for a personal protection purpose not related to performance of an official duty or status."*

Applicants must be 21 years of age or older, the age many states require an individual to be to own a firearm. Proof of compliance may include a concealed handgun license that is valid under federal, state, local or host-nation law where the DoD property is located.

"Written permission will be valid for 90 days or as long as the DoD Component deems appropriate and will include information necessary to facilitate the carrying of the firearm on DoD property consistent with safety and security, such as the individual's name, duration of the permission to carry, type of firearm, etc.,"

Without the above referenced written permission, permit holders should not take firearms onto any military base property.

# Veteran Affairs Property

No person while on property under the charge and control of VA (and not under the charge and control of the General Services Administration) shall carry firearms, other dangerous or deadly weapons, or explosives, either openly or concealed, except for official purposes.

The term "official purposes" is not defined by the federal regulation. As there is too much ambiguity about the law, permit holders should not take firearms onto Veteran Affairs Property.

Source: 38 C.F.R. § 1.218

# School Zones

The Federal Gun Free School Zone Act makes it a felony punishable by up to 5 years in prison to possess a firearm within 1,000 feet of any K-12 school in America.

**Federal Law:** *It shall be unlawful for any individual knowingly to possess a firearm that has moved in or that otherwise affects interstate or foreign commerce at a place that the individual knows, or has reasonable cause to believe, is a school zone. 18 U.S.C.A. § 922. The term "school zone" means **in, or on the grounds of, a public, parochial or private school; or within a distance of 1,000 feet from the grounds of an elementary or secondary public, parochial or private school.** 18 U.S.C.A. § 921*

There are a few exceptions to the federal law, including if:

1. You are on private property not part of school grounds;
2. You are licensed to do so **by the State in which the school zone is located** or a political subdivision of the State, and the law of the State or political subdivision requires that, before an individual obtains such a license, the law enforcement authorities of the State or political subdivision verify that the individual is qualified under law to receive the license;
3. The gun is not loaded; and in a locked container, or a locked firearms rack that is on a motor vehicle;
4. You are using the firearm in a program approved by a school in the school zone;
5. You are under a contract entered into between a school in the school zone and the individual or an employer of the individual;
6. You are a law enforcement officer acting in his or her official capacity; or

7. The gun is unloaded and is possessed by an individual while traversing school premises for the purpose of gaining access to public or private lands open to hunting, if the entry on school premises is authorized by school authorities.

The most notable exception, referenced above as #2, states that if you have a permit issued **by the state in which the school zone is located** then the federal law prohibiting firearms within 1,000 feet of a school no longer applies to you. Keep in mind, however, that this does not apply to a different state where you permit is honored (through reciprocity), but instead only to the state that issued your permit. In 2013 The US Department of Justice issued an opinion letter in which they stated the following:

> *"The law provides certain exceptions to the general ban on possession of firearms in school zones. One exception is where the individual possessing the firearm "is licensed to do so by the State in which the school zone is located or a political subdivision of the State" (title 18 U.S. C. Section 922(q)(2)(B)(ii))... the law clearly provides that in order to qualify as an exception to the general prohibition of the GFSZA, the license must be issued by the State in which the school zone is located or political subdivision of that State. A concealed weapons license or permit from any other State would not satisfied the criteria set forth in the law."*

Although this law is rarely enforced against a permit holder merely driving through a school zone in another state, it is nonetheless a serious violation of federal law and permit holders are advised to use extreme caution while traveling out of state.

Source: 18 U.S.C.A. § 922

## U.S. Army Corps of Engineers Property

Federal law prohibits the possession of loaded firearms on Corp of Engineers property unless the individual is law enforcement, is legally hunting (the gun must be unloaded to and from the hunting site), is at a firing range, or has written permission from the District Commander. Violation of these rules and regulations is a misdemeanor punishable by a fine up to $5,000, or up to six months in jail, or both. A more detailed description is below.

**36 C.F.R. 327.13**

(c) The possession of loaded firearms, ammunition, loaded projectile firing devices, bows and arrows, crossbows, or other weapons is prohibited unless:

(1) In the possession of a Federal, state or local law enforcement officer;

(2) Being used for hunting or fishing as permitted under § 327.8, with devices being unloaded when transported to, from or between hunting and fishing sites;

(3) Being used at authorized shooting ranges; or

(4) Written permission has been received from the District Commander.

(d) Possession of explosives or explosive devices of any kind, including fireworks or other pyrotechnics, is prohibited unless written permission has been received from the District Commander.

## 36 C.F.R 327.25

(a) Any person who violates the provisions of the regulations in this part... may be punished by a fine of not more than $5,000 or imprisonment for not more than six months or both and may be tried and sentenced in accordance with the provisions of section 3401 of Title 18, United States Code.

**LEGAL UPDATE:** On January 10, 2014 an Idaho federal district court issued a preliminary injunction preventing the U.S. Army Corps of Engineers ("the Corps") from enforcing the 40-year-old regulation restricting the possession of loaded firearms and ammunition on Corps-administered property. Although this case is a preliminary decision, it is likely—based upon the court's analysis—that a final injunction will issue. At that point, the Corps could appeal to the United States Court of Appeals for the Ninth Circuit. This preliminary injunction, and any final injunction that may issue, will only impact the District of Idaho. If the Ninth Circuit were to affirm, the decision would extend to Alaska, Arizona, California, Hawaii, Montana, Nevada, Oregon, and Washington. See Morris, et al.  v. United States Army Corps of Engineers.

# State Summary Pages

Each State Summary Page Contains:

* State's Constitutional Provision for the Right to Keep and Bear Arms
* State Rating - 1-5 Stars
* Issuing Authority Contact Information
* Prohibited Areas for Concealed Firearms Under State Law
* Reciprocity - what permits are honored by each state
* Statutory Citations - for quick reference checks
* Special Notes - things you need to know

# Alabama

*"That every citizen has a right to bear arms in defense of himself and the state."*

Article I §26

**Rating:** ★ ★ ★ ★

State of Alabama Attorney
General's Office
500 Dexter Avenue
Montgomery, AL 36130
(334) 242-7300

## Prohibited Areas

### Places Off Limits to Firearms Under State Law:

A person, including a person with a permit may not knowingly possess or carry a firearm in any of the following places without the express permission of a person or entity with authority over the premises (see Ala. Code § 13A-11-61.2)

1. Inside the building of a police, sheriff, or highway patrol station.

2. Inside or on the premises of a prison, jail, halfway house, community corrections facility, or other detention facility for those who have been charged with or convicted of a criminal or juvenile offense.

3. Inside or on the premises of a facility which provides inpatient or custodial care of those with psychiatric, mental, or emotional disorders.

4. Inside a courthouse, courthouse annex, a building in which a District Attorney's office is located, or a building in which a county commission or city council is currently having a regularly scheduled or specially called meeting.

5. Inside any facility hosting an athletic event not related to or involving firearms, which is sponsored by a private or public elementary or secondary school or any private or public institution of postsecondary education, unless the person has a permit issued under Section 13A-11-75(a)(1) or recognized under Section 13A-11-85.

6. Inside any facility hosting a professional athletic event not related to or involving firearms, unless the person has a permit issued under Section 13A-11-75(a)(1) or recognized under Section 13A-11-85.

7. Any building or facility to which access of unauthorized persons and prohibited articles is limited during normal hours of operation by the continuous posting of guards and the use of other security features, including, but not limited to, magnetometers, key cards, biometric screening devices, or turnstiles or other physical barriers. AL ST § 13A-11-61.2

8. Demonstrations held at a public place (having knowledge of the demonstration) (§13A-11-59). See definition of public place in the Special Notes below.

9.  Public schools (The term "public school" as used in this section applies only to a school composed of grades K-12 and shall include school buses). Ala. Code § 13A-11-72. *This prohibition does not apply to anyone with a license to carry a pistol in accordance with §13-11-75.

**Permits Recognized By This State:** ALL STATE PERMITS (Ala. Code §13A-11-85)

**Special Notes:**

**Preemption:** Alabama enacted Ala. Code § 13A-11-61.3 to give the Legislature complete control over regulation and policy pertaining to firearms, ammunition, and firearm accessories in order to ensure that such regulation and policy is applied uniformly throughout this state to each person subject to the state's jurisdiction and to ensure protection of the right to keep and bear arms recognized by the Constitutions of the State of Alabama and the United States. As such, cities and counties may not regulate the possession or carrying of firearms unless expressly authorized to do so by state law.

**Demonstration:** Demonstrating, picketing, speechmaking or marching, holding of vigils and all other like forms of conduct which involve the communication or expression of views or grievances engaged in by one or more persons, the conduct of which has the effect, intent or propensity to draw a crowd or onlookers. Such term shall not include casual use of property by visitors or tourists, which does not have an intent or propensity to attract a crowd or onlookers. (Ala. Code §13A-11-59)

*   ***Public Place* Defined.** Any place to which the general public has access and a right to resort for business, entertainment or other lawful purpose, but does not necessarily mean a place devoted solely to the uses of the public. Such term shall include the front or immediate area or parking lot of any store, shop, restaurant, tavern, shopping center or other place of business. Such term shall also include any public building, the grounds of any public building, or within the curtilage of any public building, or in any public parking lot, public street, right-of-way, sidewalk right-of-way, or within any public park or other public grounds.

**Employers:** Workers may have a gun in their car at work, if the gun remains locked in the trunk, or glove box, or other container securely affixed to vehicle, and the gun is out of sight. Ala. Code §13A-11-73.

**School Zone Exception:** *Those who possess a valid Alabama (and ONLY Alabama) concealed firearm permit may carry a firearm on the premises of a public school. (Ala. Code §13A-11-72e).

**University of Alabama:** Per University of Alabama policy firearms and other dangerous weapons are prohibited on any property owned, leased or controlled by the University. (policies.ua.edu/weapons.html). Also note that other Universities may be considering similar policy updates.

# Alaska

*"A well-regulated militia being necessary to the security of a free state, the right of the people to keep and bear arms shall not be infringed. The individual right to keep and bear arms shall not be denied or infringed by the State or a political subdivision of the State."*

Article I § 1.19

**Rating: ★ ★ ★ ★**

Alaska State Troopers
Permits and Licensing
5700 East Tudor Road
Anchorage, AK 99507-5800
(907) 269-0392

## State Prohibited Areas

**Places Off Limits to Firearms Under State Law:**

1. Any law enforcement facility (Alaska Stat. §11.61.220)

2. Public and private schools (Alaska Stat. §11.61.220)

3. Anywhere alcohol is sold for consumption (excluding restaurants if you don't drink) (Alaska Stat. §11.61.220)

4. Within the grounds of or on a parking lot immediately adjacent to an entity, other than a private residence, licensed as a child care facility under AS 47.32 or recognized by the federal government for the care of children, except that a person 21 years of age or older may possess an unloaded firearm in the trunk of a motor vehicle or encased in a closed container of a motor vehicle; (Alaska Stat. Ann. § 11.61.220)

5. Courtroom or office of the Alaska court system. (Alaska Stat. §11.61.220)

6. Domestic violence or sexual assault shelter. (Alaska Stat. §11.61.220)

7. Within another person's residence, unless the person carrying the firearm has first obtained the express permission of an adult residing there to bring the firearm into the residence. (Alaska Stat. §11.65.755)

8. Firearms and ammunition are prohibited in an assisted living home licensed for six or more residents, and in a child care center, a residential child-care facility, and a maternity home. (Alaska Admin. Code tit. 7, § 10.1080)

**Permits Recognized By This State:** ALL STATE PERMITS

**Special Notes:**

**Duty to Inform:** A person commits the crime of misconduct involving weapons in the fifth degree if the person (1) is 21 years of age or older and knowingly possesses a deadly weapon, other than an ordinary pocket knife or a defensive weapon, (A) that is concealed on the person, and, when contacted by a peace officer, the person fails to (i) immediately inform the peace officer of that possession. (Alaska Stat. §11.61.220)

# Arizona

*"The right of the individual citizen to bear arms in defense of himself or the state shall not be impaired, but nothing in this section shall be construed as authorizing individuals or corporations to organize, maintain, or employ an armed body of men."*

Article 2 §26

**Rating:** ★ ★ ★ ★

Arizona Department of
Public Safety
P. O. Box 6638
Phoenix, AZ 85005
(602) 223-2000

## Prohibited Areas

### Places Off Limits to Firearms Under State Law:

1. Any business that sells alcohol for consumption unless all 3 of the following are met:
   a. You have a CCW permit and the gun is concealed
   b. You do not consume alcohol
   c. There is not a sign prohibiting firearms posted near the liquor license Ariz. Rev. Stat. §4-229 and §4-244 (see Ariz. Rev. Stat. §13-3102 for exceptions)

2. Polling places on the day of an election Ariz. Rev. Stat. §13-3102.A.11 (see Ariz. Rev. Stat. § 13-3102.C for exceptions)

3. Public and private schools (Ariz. Rev. Stat. §13-3102.A.12) (see Ariz. Rev. Stat. §13-3102.C & J for exceptions)

4. Nuclear or hydroelectric generating facilities (Ariz. Rev. Stat. §13-3102.A.13) (see Ariz. Rev. Stat. §13-3102.C for exceptions)

5. Any "posted" buildings:
   a. Be posted in a conspicuous location accessible to the general public and immediately adjacent to the liquor license posted on the licensed premises.
   b. Contain a pictogram that shows a firearm within a red circle and a diagonal red line across the firearm.
   c. Contain the words, "no firearms allowed pursuant to A.R.S. section 4-229".

6. Correctional facilities (Ariz. Rev. Stat. §13-2505.A.1, Ariz. Rev. Stat. § 13-2514.A.1)

7. Indian reservations (Check with the tribe)

8. Military installations

9. Entering any public event after being asked to check weapon. (Ariz. Rev. Stat. §13-3102.A.10) (See Ariz. Rev. Stat. §13-3102.C & G for exceptions)

10. Interference with or disruption of an educational institution, which includes ay act that might reasonably lead to the evacuation or closure of any educational property. A.R.S. 13-2911

11. Airports secure areas (Ariz. Rev. Stat. §13-3119)

**Permits Recognized By This State:** ALL STATE PERMITS

**Special Notes:**

**Temporary Confiscation of Firearm by Law Enforcement Officer:** An officer may temporarily confiscate a firearm – even during a consensual encounter – for "Officer Safety" purposes. (Arizona v. Serna, 1 CA-CR 11-0675)

**School Exception:** The above prohibition for firearms in school zones does not apply to a: "Firearm that is not loaded and that is carried within a means of transportation under the control of an adult provided that if the adult leaves the means of transportation the firearm shall not be visible from the outside of the means of transportation and the means of transportation shall be locked." Ariz. Rev. Stat. Ann. § 13-3102.

**Municipal Restrictions:** In 1998 the city of Tucson was allowed to prohibit firearms in city parks. Tucson City Code § 21-3(5)(2) was upheld by the Arizona court of appeals. "The City ordinance which prohibited use or possession of firearms within city parks was neither preempted by nor in conflict with state firearms statutes." City of Tucson v. Rineer, 971 P.2d 207 (Ariz. App. 2d Div. 1998). Though it is a somewhat conflicting opinion, it appears that cities and municipalities have at least some ability to prohibit the carry of firearms in their jurisdictions.

**Vehicle Transport:** A.R.S. §12-781 protects the transportation or storage of firearms in locked motor vehicles or in locked motorcycle compartments on public and private parking lots, provided the firearm is not visible from outside the vehicle or motorcycle. This statutory protection does not apply to employer owned vehicles, secured parking lots with controlled access IF temporary firearm storage facilities are provided, or parking lots where specially designated alternate parking is provided for vehicles/motorcycles containing any firearms. This statutory protection does not apply to parking for single family detached residences or places where firearms are otherwise prohibited by law, e.g., federal property. A.R.S. § 12-781

# Arkansas

*"The citizens of this State shall have the right to keep and bear arms for their common defense."*

Article II Section 5

**Rating:** ★ ★ ★

Arkansas State Police
1 State Police Plaza Drive
Little Rock, AR 72209
(501) 618-8000

## Prohibited Areas

**Places Off Limits to Firearms Under State Law:**

A license to carry a concealed handgun issued under this subchapter does not authorize a person to carry a concealed handgun into:

1. Any police station, sheriff's station, or Department of Arkansas State Police station;

2. An Arkansas Highway Police Division of the Arkansas Department of Transportation facility;

3. A building of the Arkansas Department of Transportation or onto grounds adjacent to a building of the Arkansas Department of Transportation.

    a. However this section does not apply to:

        i. A rest area or weigh station of the Arkansas Department of Transportation; or

        ii. A publicly owned and maintained parking lot that is a publicly accessible parking lot if the licensee is carrying a concealed handgun in his or her motor vehicle or has left the concealed handgun in his or her locked and unattended motor vehicle in the publicly owned and maintained parking lot;

4. Any part of a detention facility, prison, or jail, including without limitation a parking lot owned, maintained, or otherwise controlled by the Department of Correction or Department of Community Correction;

5. Any courthouse, courthouse annex, or other building owned, leased, or regularly used by a county for conducting court proceedings or housing a county office unless:

    a. The licensee is either:

        i. Employed by the county;

        ii. A countywide elected official;

        iii. A justice of the peace; or

iv. Employed by a governmental entity other than the county with an office or place of employment inside the courthouse, the courthouse annex, or other building owned, leased, or regularly used by the county for conducting court proceedings or housing a county office.

6. Any courtroom.

   a. However, nothing in this subchapter precludes a judge from carrying a concealed weapon or determining who will carry a concealed weapon into his or her courtroom;

7. Any meeting place of the governing body of any governmental entity;

8. Any meeting of the General Assembly or a committee of the General Assembly;

9. Any state office;

10. Any athletic event not related to firearms;

11. A portion of an establishment, except a restaurant as defined in § 3-5-1202, licensed to dispense alcoholic beverages for consumption on the premises.

    a. A person with a concealed carry endorsement under § 5-73-322(g) and who is carrying a concealed handgun may not enter an establishment under this section if the establishment either places a written notice as permitted under subdivision (18) of this section or provides notice under subdivision (19) of this section prohibiting a person with a license to possess a concealed handgun at the physical location;

12. A portion of an establishment, except a restaurant as defined in § 3-5-1202, where beer or light wine is consumed on the premises.

    a. A person with a concealed carry endorsement under § 5-73-322(g) and who is carrying a concealed handgun may not enter an establishment under this section if the establishment either places a written notice as permitted under subdivision (18) of this section or provides notice under subdivision (19) of this section prohibiting a person with a license to possess a concealed handgun at the physical location;

13. A school, college, community college, or university campus building or event.

    a. However, this section does not apply to:

       i. A kindergarten through grade twelve (K-12) private school operated by a church or other place of worship that:

       ii. Is located on the developed property of the kindergarten through grade twelve (K-12) private school;

       iii. Allows the licensee to carry a concealed handgun into the church or other place of worship under this section; and

       iv. Allows the licensee to possess a concealed handgun on the developed property of the kindergarten through grade twelve (K-12) private school under § 5-73-119(e);

    v.  A kindergarten through grade twelve (K-12) private school or a prekindergarten private school that through its governing board or director has set forth the rules and circumstances under which the licensee may carry a concealed handgun into a building or event of the kindergarten through grade twelve (K-12) private school or the prekindergarten private school;

    vi.  Participation in an authorized firearms-related activity;

    vii.  Carrying a concealed handgun as authorized under § 5-73-322; or

    viii. A publicly owned and maintained parking lot of a college, community college, or university if the licensee is carrying a concealed handgun in his or her motor vehicle or has left the concealed handgun in his or her locked and unattended motor vehicle;

14. Inside the passenger terminal of any airport, except that no person is prohibited from carrying any legal firearm into the passenger terminal if the firearm is encased for shipment for purposes of checking the firearm as baggage to be lawfully transported on any aircraft;

15. Any church or other place of worship.

    a.  However, this subchapter does not preclude a church or other place of worship from determining who may carry a concealed handgun into the church or other place of worship.

    b.  A person with a concealed carry endorsement under § 5-73-322(g) and who is carrying a concealed handgun may not enter a church or other place of worship under this section if the church or other place of worship either places a written notice as permitted under subdivision (18) of this section or provides notice under subdivision (19) of this section prohibiting a person with a license to possess a concealed handgun at the physical location;

16. Any place where the carrying of a firearm is prohibited by federal law;

17. Any place where a parade or demonstration requiring a permit is being held, and the licensee is a participant in the parade or demonstration;

18. Any place at the discretion of the person or entity exercising control over the physical location of the place by placing at each entrance to the place a written notice clearly readable at a distance of not less than ten feet (10') that "carrying a handgun is prohibited".

    a.  Any licensee entering a private home shall notify the occupant that the licensee is carrying a concealed handgun.

19. Number 18 (above) does not apply if the place is:

    a.  A public university, public college, or community college, as defined in § 5-73-322, and the licensee is carrying a concealed handgun as provided under § 5-73-322;

    b.  A publicly owned and maintained parking lot if the licensee is carrying a concealed handgun in his or her motor vehicle or has left the concealed handgun in his or her locked and unattended motor vehicle; or

    c.  A parking lot of a private employer and the licensee is carrying a concealed handgun as provided under § 5-73-324.

d. The person or entity exercising control over the physical location of a place that does not use his, her, or its authority under this subdivision (18) to prohibit a person from possessing a concealed handgun is immune from a claim for monetary damages arising from or related to the decision not to place at each entrance to the place a written notice under this subdivision (18);

20. A place owned or operated by a private entity that prohibits the carrying of a concealed handgun that posts a written notice.

   a. A place owned or operated by a private entity that chooses not to post a written notice as described under subdivision (18)(A) of this section may provide written or verbal notification to a licensee who is carrying a concealed handgun at the place owned or operated by a private entity that carrying of a concealed handgun is prohibited.

   b. A licensee who receives written or verbal notification is deemed to have violated this law if the licensee while carrying a concealed handgun either remains at or returns to the place owned or operated by the private entity.

   c. A place owned or operated by a private entity under this subdivision includes without limitation:

      i. A private university or private college;

      ii. A church or other place of worship;

      iii. An establishment, except a restaurant as defined in § 3-5-1202, licensed to dispense alcoholic beverages for consumption on the premises; and

      iv. An establishment, except a restaurant as defined in § 3-5-1202, where beer or light wine is consumed on the premises; or

21. A posted firearm-sensitive area, as approved by the Department of Arkansas State Police under § 5-73-325, located at:

   a. The Arkansas State Hospital;

   b. The University of Arkansas for Medical Sciences; or

   c. A collegiate athletic event.

Ark. Code Ann. § 5-73-306

**Permits Recognized By This State:** ALL STATE PERMITS

## Special Notes:

**Duty to Inform:** In any official contact with law enforcement, if the licensee IS in possession of a handgun, when the officer asks the licensee for identification (driver's license, or personal information, such as name and date of birth), the licensee shall notify the officer that he or she holds a concealed handgun carry license and that he or she has a handgun in his or her possession...(Ark. Admin. Code 130.00.8-3.2(b))

**Private Homes:** Arkansas law states that any licensee entering a private home shall notify the occupant that the licensee is carrying a concealed handgun. (Ark. Code Ann. §5-73-306)

**Constitutional Carry:** On October 17, 2018 the Arkansas Court of Appeals ruled that merely possessing a weapon, with or without a permit, is not a crime in the State of Arkansas. "[I]n general merely possessing a handgun on your person ... does not violate § 5-73-120(a) and may be done if it does not violate other laws or regulations.". Under the clear language of section 5-73-120(a), the possessor of a handgun must have an unlawful intent to employ it as a weapon against a person in order to make that possession a criminal act. Taff v. State, 2018 Ark. App. 488, 9 (2018)

# California

*The California Constitution contains NO provision for the right to keep and bear arms.*

**Rating:** ★

State of California
Department of Justice
Firearms Licensing Section
P.O. Box 820200
Sacramento, CA 94203
(916) 445-9555

## Prohibited Areas

**Places Off Limits to Firearms Under State Law:**

1. Any picketing activity (Cal. Penal Code § 17510)

2. Anywhere that serves alcohol for consumption. (cannot have a firearm while consuming any alcoholic beverage or while under the influence of any medication or drug, prescribed or not)

3. Courtroom/Courthouse (Cal. Penal Code §171b(b)(2)(B))

4. Public Buildings/Meetings (see special note below)

5. Capitol or Legislative offices (Cal. Penal Code §171b(b)(3), §171c(a)(1))

6. Governor or other Constitutional Officer residences

7. Gun Shows (cannot have firearm and ammunition inside show) (Cal. Penal Code § 27330)

8. Possessing a firearm at a polling place (Cal. Elec. Code §18544(a));

9. Possessing a firearm on the buildings or grounds of the "Cal Expo" center in Sacramento (Cal. Code Regs. tit. 14, § 4955);

10. School Grounds, including colleges and universities.  Cal. Penal Code § 30310

11. California State Parks (Cal. Code Regs. Tit. 14, §4313(a)). (Firearms that do not have a cartridge in any portion of the mechanism, or other unloaded weapons, may be possessed within temporary lodging or a mechanical mode of conveyance when such weapons are rendered temporarily inoperable or are packed, cased, or stored in a manner that will prevent their ready use. Section 4313(c). )

12. Possessing a firearm in or on the buildings or grounds of:

    a. A childcare center (Cal. Code Regs. tit. 22, § 101238(g)(2));

    b. A social rehabilitation facility (Cal. Code Regs. tit. 22, § 81087(g));

    c. The residences of transitional housing placement program licensees (Cal. Code Regs. tit. 22, 86087(d)); or

    d. Crisis nurseries (Cal. Code Regs. tit. 22, § 86587(g)(2)).

**Permits Recognized By This State: NONE**

## Special Notes:

**Duty to Inform:** California's duty to inform is not specified in state code, but is instead instituted on a county-by-county basis. Accordingly, Legal Heat recommends assuming there is an affirmative duty to inform

**Large Capacity Magazines Prohibited:** It is illegal for any person to import into the state any large-capacity magazine. (see Cal. Penal Code § 32310). A "Large Capacity Magazine" is defined as any ammunition-feeding device with the capacity to accept more than 10 rounds. Cal. Penal Code § 16740.

- On August 14, 2020 the Ninth Circuit court of appeals affirmed a lower court ruling, which overturned California's Large Capacity Magazine (LCM) ban (Penal Code section 32310). The court ruled that firearm magazines are "arms" protected by the Second Amendment, as many weapons would be useless, including quintessential self-defense weapons like the handgun, without a magazine. Although excellent, this ruling currently has a stay in place, which means the final ruling will not take effect until all appeals are heard. This process may take years, and until that time the LCM ban is still in effect. Duncan v. Becerra, 970 F.3d 1133, 1141 (9th Cir. 2020).

**Loaded vs. Unloaded:** California also prohibits any individual, without a permit, from carrying a loaded firearm of any kind on his or her person or in a vehicle while in any public place or on any public street in an incorporated city, or in any public place or on any public street in a prohibited area of unincorporated territory. Section 12031(a)(1). "Loaded" in this context means that the firearm has a cartridge or shell in a chamber, clip or magazine that is in or attached in some way to the firearm. Section 12031(g).

**Public Buildings:** Licensees are EXEMPT from the prohibition of carry onto state or local public buildings. Subject to several exceptions, a "public building" is: (1) It is a building or part of a building owned or leased by the state or local government, if state or local public employees are regularly present for the purposes of performing their official duties. A state or local public building includes, but is not limited to, a building that contains a courtroom. (2) It is not a building or facility, or a part thereof that is referred to in Section 171c, 171d, 626.9, 626.95, or 626.10 of this code, or in Section 18544 of the Elections Code. (3) It is a building not regularly used, and not intended to be used, by state or local employees as a place of residence. Cal. Penal Code Ann. § 171b

**Vehicles:** California also prohibits any individual from carrying a loaded firearm of any kind on his or her person or in a vehicle while in any public place or on any public street in an incorporated city, or in any public place or on any public street in a prohibited area of unincorporated territory. Section 12031(a)(1). "Loaded" in this context means that the firearm has a cartridge or shell in a chamber, clip or magazine that is in or attached in some way to the firearm. Section 12031(g).

## Colorado

*"The right of no person to keep and bear arms in defense of his home, person and property, or in aid of the civil power when thereto legally summoned, shall be called in question; but nothing herein contained shall be construed to justify the practice of carrying concealed weapons."*

Article II §13

**Rating: ★ ★ ★**

Colorado Bureau of
Investigation
690 Kipling Street, Suite 3000
Denver, CO 80215
(303) 239-4201

## Prohibited Areas

**Places Off Limits to Firearms Under State Law:**

1. Any building in which the chambers, galleries, or offices of the general assembly, or either house thereof, are located, or in which a legislative hearing or meeting is being or is to be conducted, or in which the official office of any member, officer, or employee of the general assembly is located. (Colo. Rev. Stat. §18-12-105 (c)) (Permit holders are exempt from this prohibition).

2. Public and private schools (A permittee may have a handgun on the real property of the public school so long as the handgun remains in his or her vehicle and, if the permittee is not in the vehicle, the handgun is in a compartment within the vehicle and the vehicle is locked) (Colo. Rev. Stat. §18-12-214(3)(a))

3. Posted buildings. Nothing shall be construed to limit, restrict, or prohibit in any manner the existing rights of a private property owner, private tenant, private employer, or private business entity.  (Colo. Rev. Stat. §18-12-214(5)). (See also Colo A.G. Opinion June 17, 2003)

4. Any building where Security personnel and electronic weapons screening devices are permanently in place at each entrance to the building. (Colo. Rev. Stat. §18-12-214(4))

5. Any public transportation facility. (Colo. Rev. Stat. §18-9-118) (only a crime when done "without legal authority" – a permit would likely be legal authority)

6. Buildings With Metal Detectors: No person, regardless of a permit to carry a concealed handgun, may carry a concealed handgun into a public building at which security personnel and electronic screening devices are permanently in place at each entrance, each person entering the building is screened, and persons carrying weapons are required to leave them with security while in the building. (Colo. Rev. Stat. §29-11.7-104)

**Permits Recognized By This State:** Alabama, Alaska, Arizona, Arkansas, Delaware, Florida, Georgia, Idaho, Iowa, Indiana, Kansas, Kentucky, Louisiana, Michigan, Mississippi, Missouri, Montana, Nebraska, New Hampshire, New Mexico, North Carolina, North Dakota, Ohio, Oklahoma, Pennsylvania, South Dakota, Tennessee, Texas, Utah, Virginia, West Virginia, Wisconsin, Wyoming (Colorado Only Honors Permits Held by Residents of the Above States).

## Special Notes:

**Large Capacity Magazines:** Colorado defines large capacity magazines to include any fixed or detachable device that holds 15+. The definition also includes limits on shotguns. For shotguns, if the magazine is tubular, you cannot hold more than 28 inches of shells, and if it's non-tubular, it cannot be capable of accepting more than 8 shells. (Colo. Rev. Stat. §18-12-301(2)(a)). The law bans the sale, transfer, and possession of large capacity of magazines. However, if you owned the magazine before the effective date (July 1, 2013), you may still possess it. (Colo. 18-12-302(1)(a) & (2)(a).

**Vehicle Carry:** Colorado law allows for the carry of firearms (loaded or unloaded) in a vehicle with or without a permit so long as they are carried for "lawful protection of a person or property". C.R.S. 18-12-105

**Posted Buildings:** There has been some debate as to whether "Posted Buildings" have force of law in Colorado. When discussing what areas are off limits to firearms, the applicable Colorado law states: *(5) Nothing...shall be construed to limit, restrict, or prohibit in any manner the existing rights of a private property owner, private tenant, private employer, or private business entity.* (See Colo. Rev. Stat. Ann §18-12-214) In specifically interpreting the above statute, the Colorado Attorney General stated: *"The concealed weapons law does not restrict the rights of private property owners, tenants, employers or businesses to control the carrying of concealed handguns onto their premises."* 2003 WL 21770953 (Colo. A.G. June 17, 2003). Some jurisdictions, like Aurora, have enacted ordinances that make the carrying into  posted buildings illegal (see Sec. 94-152). Use caution with Colorado posted buildings

**Police Stops:** A peace officer may temporarily disarm a permittee, incident to a lawful stop of the permittee. The peace officer shall return the handgun to the permittee prior to discharging the permittee from the scene. Colo. Rev. Stat. Ann. § 18-12-214

**Statewide Preemption:** C.R.S. 18-12-214(1)(a): A permit to carry a concealed handgun authorizes the permittee to carry a concealed handgun in all areas of the state, except as specifically limited in this section. A local government does not have authority to adopt or enforce an ordinance or resolution that would conflict with any provision of this part.

**Snowmobiles:** It is unlawful to operate or ride on any snowmobile with any firearm in his or her possession, unless such firearm is unloaded and enclosed in a carrying case or inserted in a scabbard, or with any bow unless it is unstrung or cased. Colo. Rev. Stat. Ann. § 33-14-117

# Connecticut

*"Every citizen has a right to bear arms in defense of himself and the state."*

Article I §15

**Rating:** ★ ★ ★

Connecticut State Police
Special Licensing & Firearms Unit
P.O. Box 2794
Middletown, CT 06457
(860) 685-8000

## Prohibited Areas

**Places Off Limits to Firearms Under State Law:**

1. Primary and secondary schools or school sponsored activities (Unless approved by school officials) (Conn. Gen. Stat. §53a-217b)

2. Posted "No Guns Allowed" buildings. (Conn. Gen. Stat. §29-28)

3. State park or forests. (Conn. Gen. Stat. §23-4-1(c)); (even while hunting)

4. Any building in which the official office of any member, officer or employee of the General Assembly or the office of any committee of the General Assembly is located. (Conn. Gen. Stat. §2-1e)

5. Courthouses.

6. Any place a legislative committee is holding a public hearing

7. Anywhere a committee of the General Assembly is holding a public hearing. (Conn. Gen. Stat. §2-1e(c))

8. A state administrative regulation states that possession of a dangerous weapon in a shelter for the homeless constitutes good cause for expulsion or suspension from the shelter. Conn. Agencies Regs. §17-590-5. Similarly, possession of firearms on the grounds of the Connecticut Department of Veteran Affairs constitutes cause for an immediate involuntary discharge from programs administered by that Department. (Conn. Gen. Stat. §27-102l(d)-132)

9. Administrative regulations also prohibit firearms:

    a. In any state park or forest except as authorized by the Department of Environmental Protection (Conn. Agencies Regs. §23-4-1(c))

    b. In Bluff Point Coastal Preserve, except for certain authorized persons (Conn. Agencies Regs. §23-4-4(B)(3))

    c. Inside of or within 50 feet of any magazine or in or around any trucks or other vehicles containing explosives (Conn. Agencies Regs. §29-349-135, §29-349-198)

    d. Inside or within 50 feet of any plant, area, or warehouse used for mixing, packaging, or storing blasting agents (Conn. Agencies Regs. §29-349-274)

10. WoodBridge, CT has the following city ordinance prohibiting firearms:
   a. § 231-3. Town property. A. No person shall possess a firearm, air gun, air rifle, or crossbow, longbow, archery equipment, or other weapon on any Town-owned property and/or in Town-owned buildings, except any lawful possession of firearms on roads, highways, and streets within the Town shall be permitted.

**Permits Recognized By This State: NONE**

## Special Notes:

**Large Capacity Magazines:** Connecticut law bans possession of magazines that hold more than ten rounds. There are some exceptions that allow you to have one registered large capacity magazine, but that magazine can only contain 10 rounds, and must be housed in the firearm. You cannot carry a large capacity spare magazine, even if only 10 rounds are in it. (Conn. Gen. Stat. Ann. P.A 13-3, §§ 23 & 24)

**Police Encounters - Quasi Duty to inform:** The holder of a permit shall carry such permit upon one's person while carrying such pistol or revolver. Such holder shall present his or her permit **upon the request of a law enforcement** officer who has reasonable suspicion of a crime for purposes of verification of the validity of the permit or identification of the holder, **provided such holder is carrying a pistol or revolver that is observed by such law enforcement officer.** Conn. Gen. Stat. Ann. § 29-35

**Negligent storage of a firearm:** A person is guilty of criminally negligent storage of a firearm when he violates the provisions of section 29-37i and a minor obtains the firearm and causes the injury or death of himself or any other person. For the purposes of this section, "minor" means any person under the age of sixteen years. (b) The provisions of this section shall not apply if the minor obtains the firearm as a result of an unlawful entry to any premises by any person. (c) Criminally negligent storage of a firearm is a class D felony. (Conn. Gen. Stat. §53a-217a)

**Storage of Firearm in Vehicle**: No person shall store or keep any pistol or revolver in any motor vehicle that is unattended unless such pistol or revolver is in the trunk, a locked safe or locked glove box. For purposes of this law, a motor vehicle is "unattended" if no person who is at least twenty-one years of age and who is the owner or operator or a passenger of such motor vehicle is inside the motor vehicle or is within close enough proximity to the motor vehicle to prevent unauthorized access to the motor vehicle. Conn. Gen. Stat. Ann. § P.A. 19-7, § 1

**No Preemption:** Connecticut does not have preemptive laws, thus a city or municipality may impose additional restrictions on the carry of concealed firearms. Check with each municipality prior to carrying.

# Delaware

*"A person has the right to keep and bear arms for the defense of self, family, home and State, and for hunting and recreational use."*

Art. I, § 20

**Rating:** ★ ★

State of Delaware
Office of the Attorney General
Carvel State Office Building
820 North French Street
Wilmington, DE 19801

## Prohibited Areas

**Places Off Limits to Firearms Under State Law:**

1. Courthouses, Police Stations, Prisons and other "Detention Facilities" (Del. Code Ann. tit.11, §1256, §1258)

2. It shall be unlawful for any person to possess a firearm within Division offices, visitor centers, nature centers, educational facilities, facilities or locations used for authorized special events or festivals, and maintenance shops, (and shall be identified by appropriate signage), except as authorized by the Director in writing. Code Del. Regs. 7 3000 3900 (8.3.4.1)

3. The City of Dover requires a CCDW or state permit with reciprocity to open or conceal carry (Dover Ordinance 14-5).

4. Del. Code Ann. tit.11, §1256 prohibits knowingly and unlawfully introducing contraband (defined by Del. Code Ann. tit.11, §1258 to include firearms) into a detention facility. That section also prohibits a person confined in a detention facility from knowingly and unlawfully making, obtaining, or possessing contraband. A "detention facility" is any place used to confine a person pursuant to court order. (Del. Code Ann. tit.11, §1258)

5. A state administrative regulation also prohibits weapons of any kind on a school bus. (14-1100-1105 Del. Code Regs. §6.14)

6. Group homes for persons with mental illness (40-300-004 Del. Code Regs. § 61.1307)

7. Neighborhood homes for persons with developmental disabilities (40-300-008 Del. Code Regs. § 55.1106)

**Permits Recognized By This State:** Alaska, Arkansas, Arizona, Colorado, Florida, Idaho (enhanced permit only), Kentucky, Maine, Michigan, Missouri, New Mexico, North Carolina, North Dakota (Class 1 Permits Only), Ohio, Oklahoma, South Dakota (Enhanced Permit Only), Tennessee, Texas, Utah, West Virginia

## Special Notes:

**Quasi Duty to Inform:** One carrying a weapon must inform law enforcement of the weapon when asked if they are in possession of any weapons. (see *Griffin v. State*, 47 A.3d 487)

**Gun Ban in State Parks is Unconstitutional:** On 12/7/17 the Delaware Supreme Court ruled that a regulation banning guns in state parks and forests is unconstitutional and in contravention to Delawareans' rights. Bridgeville Rifle & Pistol Club, Ltd. v. Small, No. 15, 2017, 2017 WL 6048843, at *1 (Del. Dec. 7, 2017)

# Florida

*"The right of the people to keep and bear arms in defense of themselves and of the lawful authority of the state shall not be infringed, except that the manner of bearing arms may be regulated by law."*

Art. I §8

**Rating:** ★ ★ ★ ★

Division of Licensing
Department of Agriculture &
Consumer Services
P.O. Box 6687
Tallahassee, FL 32314

## Prohibited Areas

### Places Off Limits to Firearms Under State Law:

1. Any place of nuisance as defined in Fla. Stat. §823.05 (Fla. Stat. §790.06(12))

2. Any police, sheriff, or highway patrol station (Fla. Stat. §790.06(12))

3. Any detention facility, prison, or jail; any courthouse (Fla. Stat. §790.06(12))

4. Any courtroom, except with judge's permission (Fla. Stat. §790.06(12))

5. Any polling place (Fla. Stat. §790.06(12))

6. Any meeting of the governing body of a county, public school district, municipality, or special district. (Fla. Stat. §790.06(12))

7. Any meeting of the Legislature or a committee thereof. (Fla. Stat. §790.06(12))

8. Any school, college, or professional athletic event not related to firearms. (Fla. Stat. §790.06(12))

9. Any school administration building (Fla. Stat. §790.06(12))

10. Any portion of an establishment licensed to dispense alcoholic beverages for consumption (Portion primarily devoted to such purpose) (Fla. Stat. §790.06(12))

11. Any elementary or secondary school facility (Fla. Stat. §790.06(12))

12. Any career center (Fla. Stat. §790.06(12))

13. Any college or university facility unless the licensee is a registered student, employee, or faculty member of such college or university and the weapon is a stun gun or non-lethal electric weapon or device designed solely for defensive purposes and the weapon does not fire a dart or projectile (Fla. Stat. §790.06(12))

14. Any Seaport Security area. (Fla. Stat. § 311.12)

15. In Savannas State Reserve. (Fla. Stat. § 258.157).

16. Any hospital providing mental health services, including "into or upon the grounds" of such hospital.  Fla. Stat. Ann. § 394.458

**Permits Recognized By This State:** Alabama, Alaska, Arizona, Arkansas, Colorado, Delaware, Georgia, Idaho, Indiana, Iowa, Kansas, Kentucky, Louisiana, Maine, Michigan, Mississippi, Missouri, Montana, Nebraska, New Hampshire, Nevada, New Mexico, North Carolina, North Dakota, Ohio, Oklahoma, Pennsylvania, South Carolina, South Dakota, Tennessee, Texas, Utah, Vermont, West Virginia, Wyoming **(Florida Only Recognizes Permits Held By Residents Of The Above States)**.

## Special Notes:

**Police Encounters:** Florida is a **quasi duty to inform** state, which means that you are not affirmatively required to tell a police officer that you have a firearm in your possession, but if you are asked by an officer during a lawful stop you must provide them with your permit and photo identification card.

- **The Law**: A licensee must carry the license, together with valid identification, at all times in which the licensee is in actual possession of a concealed weapon or firearm and must display both the license and proper identification upon demand by a law enforcement officer. Fla. Stat. Ann. § 790.06

**Employers:** No public or private employer may prohibit any customer, employee, or invitee from possessing any legally owned firearm when such firearm is lawfully possessed and locked inside or locked to a private motor vehicle in a parking lot and when the customer or employee is lawfully in such area. (Fla. Stat. §790.251(4)(a))

**Open Carry Prohibited:** Except as otherwise provided by law it is unlawful for any person to openly carry on or about his or her person any firearm or electric weapon or device. It is not a violation of this section for a person licensed to carry a concealed firearm, and who is lawfully carrying a firearm in a concealed manner, to briefly and openly display the firearm to the ordinary sight of another person, unless the firearm is intentionally displayed in an angry or threatening manner, not in necessary self-defense. Fla. Stat. Ann. § 790.053

**School Parking Lots:** As a general rule, one may keep a firearm in a vehicle in the parking lot of a school (Fla. Stat. §790.115). However, it is important to note that Florida law does allow for schools to adopt policies that prohibit keeping guns in one's vehicle on school property for purposes of student and campus parking privileges pursuant to Fla. Stat. §790.25(5).   *As of Dec. 26, 2013, a public University cannot enforce rules that prohibit students or faculty from storing firearms in their vehicles on College/University property.  But for private colleges and universities, though it isn't criminal, they can fire and expel for violating private school rules related to firearm storage on their property. (*Lainez v. University of North Florida*, District Court of Appeal First District, State of Florida, Case No. 1D12-2174).

## Georgia

*"The right of the people to keep and bear arms shall not be infringed, but the General Assembly shall have power to prescribe the manner in which arms may be borne."*

Art. I, § 1, ¶ VIII

**Rating:** ★ ★ ★

Georgia Department of Law
Office of the Attorney General
Public Safety Section
40 Capitol Square, SW
Atlanta, GA 30334
(404) 656-4585

## Prohibited Areas

**Places Off Limits to Firearms Under State Law:**

A person shall be guilty of carrying a weapon or long gun in an unauthorized location and punished as for a misdemeanor when he or she carries a weapon or long gun while (see Ga. Code Ann. § 16-11-127):

1. In a government building as a non license holder;

2. In a courthouse;

3. In a jail or prison;

4. In a place of worship, unless the governing body or authority of the place of worship permits the carrying of weapons or long guns by license holders;

5. In a state mental health facility as defined in Code Section 37-1-1 which admits individuals on an involuntary basis for treatment of mental illness, developmental disability, or addictive disease; provided, however, that carrying a weapon or long gun in such location in a manner in compliance with paragraph (3) of subsection (d) of this Code section shall not constitute a violation of this subsection;

6. On the premises of a nuclear power facility, except as provided in Code Section 16-11-127.2, and the punishment provisions of Code Section 16-11-127.2 shall supersede the punishment provisions of this Code section; or

7. Within 150 feet of any polling place when elections are being conducted and such polling place is being used as a polling place.

8. Posted Businesses: Private property owners or persons in legal control of private property through a lease, rental agreement, licensing agreement, contract, or any other agreement to control access to such private property shall have the right to exclude or eject a person who is in possession of a weapon or long gun on their private property. A violation of this Code section shall not create or give rise to a civil action for damages. Ga. Code Ann. § 16-11-127.

9. Schools: It shall be unlawful for any person to carry to or to possess or have under such person's control while within a school safety zone or at a school function, or on a bus or other transportation furnished by a school any weapon. Any license holder who violates this subsection shall be guilty of a misdemeanor. (See exceptions in Special Notes) Ga. Code Ann. § 16-11-127.1

**The above Prohibited Areas do not apply to:**

A weapon or long gun possessed by a license holder which is under the possessor's control in a motor vehicle or is in a locked compartment of a motor vehicle or one which is in a locked container in or a locked firearms rack which is on a motor vehicle and such vehicle is parked in a parking facility.

**Permits Recognized By This State:** Alabama, Alaska, Arkansas, Arizona, Colorado, Florida, Idaho, Indiana, Iowa, Kansas, Kentucky, Louisiana, Maine Michigan, Mississippi, Missouri, Montana, New Hampshire, North Carolina, North Dakota, Ohio, Oklahoma, Pennsylvania, South Dakota, Tennessee, Texas, Utah, Virginia, West Virginia, Wisconsin, Wyoming.

## Special Notes:

**School Exception:** The firearm prohibition on school grounds shall not apply to:

a. Any weapons carry license holder when he or she is in any building or on real property owned by or leased to any public technical school, vocational school, college, or university, or other public institution of postsecondary education; provided, however, that such exception shall:

b. Not apply to buildings or property used for athletic sporting events or student housing, including, but not limited to, fraternity and sorority houses;

c. Not apply to any preschool or childcare space located within such buildings or real property;

d. Not apply to any room or space being used for classes related to a college and career academy or other specialized school as provided for under Code Section 20-4-37;

e. Not apply to any room or space being used for classes in which high school students are enrolled through a dual enrollment program, including, but not limited to, classes related to the "Move on When Ready Act" as provided for under Code Section 20-2-161.3;

f. Not apply to faculty, staff, or administrative offices or rooms where disciplinary proceedings are conducted;

g. Only apply to the carrying of handguns which a licensee is licensed to carry pursuant to subsection (e) of Code Section 16-11-126 and pursuant to Code Section 16-11-129; and

h. Only apply to the carrying of handguns which are concealed.

Any weapons carry license holder who carries a handgun in a manner or in a building, property, room, or space in violation of this paragraph shall be guilty of a misdemeanor; provided, however, that for a conviction of a first offense, such weapons carry license holder shall be punished by a fine of $25.00 and not be sentenced to serve any term of confinement. Ga. Code Ann. § 16-11-127.1

**Government Buildings:** A license holder shall be authorized to carry a weapon in a government building when the government building is open for business and where ingress into such building is not restricted or screened by security personnel. A license holder who enters or attempts to enter a government building carrying a weapon where ingress is restricted or screened by security personnel shall be guilty of a misdemeanor if at least one member of such security personnel is certified as a peace officer pursuant to Chapter 8 of Title 35; provided, however, that a license holder who immediately exits such building or immediately leaves such location upon notification of his or her failure to clear security due to the carrying of a weapon shall not be guilty. Ga. Code Ann. § 16-11-127

**Parks and Historic Sites:** Any person with a valid weapons carry license may carry a weapon in all parks, historic sites, or recreational areas, as such term is defined in Code Section 12-3-10, including all publicly owned buildings located in such parks, historic sites, and recreational areas, in wildlife management areas, and on public transportation; provided, however, that a person shall not carry a handgun into a place where it is prohibited by federal law. Ga. Code Ann. § 16-11-126

# Hawaii

*"A well regulated militia being necessary to the security of a free state, the right of the people to keep and bear arms shall not be infringed."*

Art. I, § 17

**Rating:** ★

State of Hawaii
Office of the Attorney General
Criminal Justice Division
425 Queen Street
Honolulu, HI 96813
(808) 586-1282

## Prohibited Areas

### Places Off Limits to Firearms Under State Law:

1. No person may enter a sterile area, or board or attempt to board an air carrier aircraft while possessing on or about his or her person (including in carry-on baggage) any firearm, explosive or incendiary device. (Haw. Code R. §19-14-3(e)) This provision makes no exception for concealed weapons license holders.

2. Hawaii prohibits any person from carrying or possessing a loaded firearm on any public highway. (Haw. Rev. Stat.§134-26(a)). This prohibition does not apply to any person who has in his or her possession a handgun while licensed per section 134-9. (Haw. Rev. Stat. §134-26(a))

**Permits Recognized By This State: NONE**

### Special Notes:

**Large Capacity Magazine:** Hawaii bans the possession, sale, or transfer of all magazines containing 10+ rounds. (Haw. Rev. Stat. § 134-8(c)).

**No Known Permits:** Although Hawaii does have a provision that allows for concealed carry permits to be issued, no permits have been issued to our knowledge.

**Where Carry is Allowed:** Firearms and ammunition generally must be confined to the possessor's place of business, residence or sojourn, but the possessor may carry unloaded firearms or ammunition in an enclosed container from the place of purchase to the person's place of business, residence or sojourn, or between these places upon change of place of business, residence, or sojourn, or between these places and a:

- Place of repair; Target range; Licensed dealer's place of business; Organized, scheduled firearms show or exhibit; Place of formal hunter or firearm use training or instruction; or Police station. (See Haw. Rev. Stat. §134-23(a), 134-24(a), 134-25(a), 134-27(a)).

# Idaho

*"The people have the right to keep and bear arms, which right shall not be abridged; but this provision shall not prevent the passage of laws to govern the carrying of weapons concealed on the person... No law shall impose licensure, registration or special taxation on the ownership or possession of firearms or ammunition. Nor shall any law permit the confiscation of firearms, except those actually used in the commission of a felony."*

Art. I, § 11

**Rating:** ★ ★ ★ ★ ★

State of Idaho
Office of the Attorney General
Statehouse
Boise, ID 83720

## Prohibited Areas

### Places Off Limits to Firearms Under State Law:

1. Courthouses (Idaho Code Ann. §18-3302C(1))
2. Juvenile and adult correctional facilities (Idaho Code Ann. §18-3302C(1))
3. Public and private schools (Idaho Code Ann. §18-3302C(1))

### Permits Recognized By This State: ALL STATE PERMITS

### Special Notes:

**Constitutional Carry:** Effective July 1, 2020 Idaho now has constitutional (or permitless) carry for anyone who is: 1) Over eighteen (18) years of age; 2) A citizen of the United States or a current member of the armed forces of the United States; and 3) would not otherwise be disqualified from being issued a concealed permit. Idaho Code Ann. § 18-3302(4)(f)

**School Property Exception**: The prohibition against possessing a firearm on school property (K-12) does not apply to:

- Any adult over eighteen (18) years of age and not enrolled in a public or private elementary or secondary school who has lawful possession of a firearm or other deadly or dangerous weapon, secured and locked in his vehicle in an unobtrusive, nonthreatening manner...A person who lawfully possesses a firearm or other deadly or dangerous weapon in a private vehicle while delivering minor children, students or school employees to and from school or a school activity; Idaho Code Ann. § 18-3302D.

## Enhanced Permit:

- Effective 07-01-13 Idaho began issuing an "Enhanced Permit" to those who wish to complete 8 hours of training involving 98 rounds of live fire. These enhanced permits are designed to increase the reciprocity of the Idaho permit, though the actual increase in reciprocity will not be known for several years. (See Idaho Code Ann. 18-3302(k))

## University Campus Carry:

- Those who possess an Idaho Enhanced Permit may carry their firearm onto public university or college campuses except within (1) a student dormitory or residence hall; or (2) Within any building of a public entertainment facility, provided that proper signage is conspicuously posted at each point of public ingress to the facility notifying attendees of any restriction on the possession of firearms in the facility during the game or event. A "Public entertainment facility" means an arena, stadium, amphitheater, auditorium, theater or similar facility with a seating capacity of at least one thousand (1,000) persons. Idaho Code Ann. § 18-3309.

## Posted Buildings:

- It should be noted that the Attorney General of Idaho has made the following statement on his website: May I carry a concealed weapon in private businesses that are open to the public? "Yes, unless the private business, which is open to the public forbids carrying weapons on the business premises. Private businesses are within their rights to prohibit weapons on their property." This does not mean posted buildings is illegal in Idaho, it simply means they may ask you to leave if they disagree with you carrying.

## Must Possess Permit:

- While in Idaho, a permitee must have a valid permit on his or her person at all times while carrying a firearm. (§18-3302(12)(g))

# Illinois

*"Subject only to the police power, the right of the individual citizen to keep and bear arms shall not be infringed."*

Art. I, § 22

**Rating:** ★ ★

## Prohibited Areas

### Places Off Limits to Firearms Under State Law:

Concealed carry is prohibited in the following locations:

1. Any building, real property, and parking area under the control of a public or private elementary or secondary school.

2. Any building, real property, and parking area under the control of a pre-school or child care facility.

3. Any building, real property, and parking area under the control of the executive or legislative branches (this excludes DNR parks).

4. Any building designated for matters before a circuit court, or any building or portion of a building under the control of the Supreme Court.

5. Any building or portion of a building under the control of a unit of local government.

6. Any building, real property, and parking area under the control of an adult or juvenile detention facility, correctional institution, prison, or jail.

7. Any building, real property, and parking area under the control of a public or private hospital, mental health facility, or nursing home.

8. Any bus, train, or form of transportation paid for in whole or in part with public funds, and any building, real property, and parking area under the control of a public transportation facility.

9. Any building, real property, and parking area under the control of an establishment that serves alcohol on its premises IF more than 50% of the establishment's gross receipts within the prior 3 months is from the sale of alcohol.

10. Any public gathering or special event conducted on property open to the public that requires the issuance of a permit from the unit of local government, provided this prohibition shall not apply to a licensee who must walk through a public gathering in order to access his or her residence, place of business, or vehicle.

11. Any building or real property that has been issued a special event retailer's license designated for the sale of alcohol.

12. Any public playground

13. Any public park, athletic area, or athletic facility under the control of a municipality or park district (excluding while on a trail or bikeway if only a portion of the trail or bikeway includes a public park).

14. Any real property under the control of the Cook County Forest Preserve District.

15. Any building, classroom, laboratory, medical clinic, hospital, artistic venue, athletic venue, entertainment venue, officially recognized university related organization property, and any real property, including parking areas, sidewalks, and common areas under the control of a public or private community college, college, or university.

16. Any building, real property, and parking area under the control of a gaming facility.

17. Any stadium, arena, or the real property or parking area under the control of a stadium, arena, or any collegiate or professional sporting event.

18. Any building, real property, and parking area under the control of a public library.

19. Any building, real property, and parking area under the control of an airport.

20. Any building, real property, and parking area under the control of an amusement park.

21. Any building, real property, and parking area under the control of a zoo or museum.

22. Anywhere on OR AROUND the property of a nuclear facility (no parking near).

23. Posted buildings or property with signs conspicuously posted by the owner.

**Permits Recognized By This State: NONE**

## Special Notes:

**Police Encounters** - Quasi Duty to Inform: Illinois is a quasi duty to inform state, which means that you are not affirmatively required to tell a police officer that you have a firearm in your possession, but if you are asked by an officer during a lawful stop you must provide them with your permit.

- **The Law**: If an officer of a law enforcement agency initiates an investigative stop, including but not limited to a traffic stop, of a licensee or a non-resident carrying a concealed firearm, **upon the request of the officer the licensee or non-resident shall disclose to the officer that he or she is in possession of a concealed firearm, present the license upon the request of the officer if he or she is a licensee.** During a traffic stop, any passenger within the vehicle who is a licensee or a non-resident carrying must comply with the requirements of this subsection. 430 ILCS 66/10

**Large Capacity Magazine:** Illinois has several city ordinances regulating large capacity magazines for rifles, but none for handguns.

**Non-Resident Citizens Allowed to Apply for CCL:** Illinois limits which non-residents may apply for a CCL by state. Right now, only citizens of Hawaii may apply for an Illinois CCL.

**TRANSPORTATION OF A FIREARM:**

- **Illinois Resident <u>Without</u> a Permit:** As an Illinois resident, transporting a firearm in a vehicle is only allowed if the firearm is
(i) broken down in a non-functioning state; or (ii) not immediately accessible; or (iii) unloaded and enclosed in a case, firearm carrying box, shipping box, or other container by a person who has been issued a currently valid Firearm Owner's Identification Card. IL ST CH 720 § 5/24-1.6

- **Non-Resident <u>With</u> Any Permit:** Out of state residents are granted a limited exception to lawfully carry a concealed firearm within a vehicle if they are eligible to carry a firearm in public under the laws of his or her state or territory of residence and are not prohibited from owning or possessing a firearm under federal law. If the non-resident leaves his/her vehicle unattended, he or she shall store the firearm within a locked vehicle or locked container within the vehicle in accordance with subsection (b) of Section 65 of the Firearm Concealed Carry Act.

- **Non-Resident <u>Without</u> Any Permits:** Without a permit, non-residents must have the gun in a case. Additionally, the firearm must not be immediately accessible or must be broken down in a non-functioning state. (720 IL ST CH §5/24-1)

# Indiana

*"The people shall have a right to bear arms, for the defense of themselves and the State."*

Art.I §3

**Rating:** ★ ★ ★ ★

## Prohibited Areas

**Places Off Limits to Firearms Under State Law:**

1. In a commercial or charter aircraft (Ind. Code § 35-47-6-1)

2. In an area of an airport where access is controlled by the inspection of persons and property (Ind. Code § 35-47-6-1.3)

3. In or on school property (including private schools and preschools; see Ind. Code §35-41-1-24.7) (Ind. Code §35-47-9-2)

4. In or on property that is being used by a school for a school function or on a school bus (Ind. Code §35-47-9-2)

5. On board a riverboat gambling operation (68 Ind. Admin. Code 1-7-1)

6. On the fairgrounds during the annual state fair (80 Ind. Admin. Code 4-4-4(b); any person properly licensed to carry a firearm must secure the firearm in a locked compartment of his or her vehicle, where it will not be visible, per 80 Ind. Admin. Code 4-4-4(d))

7. In or on port areas or port property (130 Ind. Admin. Code 4-1-7 and 4-1-8(2))

8. Licensees also cannot carry in children's homes and child caring institutions run or overseen by Child Welfare Services. (465 Ind. Admin. Code 2-9-80(b)(3); 465 Ind. Admin. Code 2-10-79(b)(3); 465 Ind. Admin. Code 2-11-80(b)(3); 465 Ind. Admin. Code 2-12-78(b)(3); 465 Ind. Admin. Code 2-13-77(b)(3)). In addition, childcare centers must prominently post in places regularly viewed by parents' prohibitions against the use or possession of firearms, unless such possession is required as a condition of employment. (470 Ind. Admin Code 3-4.7-19(a)(5)(C))

9. A reservoir owned by the U.S. Army Corps of Engineers, DNR property* or Falls of Ohio State Park, unless unloaded and in a case or locked vehicle... (312 Ind. Admin Code 8-2-3 & 312 Ind. Admin. Code 8-2-3)

10. On State Fair property during the State Fair, unless locked in a vehicle concealed from view. (80 IAC 4-4-4).

**Permits Recognized By This State:** ALL STATE PERMITS

## Special Notes:

**Must Carry Permit:** Although the wording of the law (and applicable caselaw) is ambiguous, it appears Ind. Code Ann. § 35-47-2-1 requires a permit holder to have in his/ her permit in his/her possession at all times while carrying.

**Open Carry:** *Does Indiana statute require me to carry the handgun on my person concealed or exposed?* Indiana law is silent on this issue; however, carrying an exposed weapon in public may alarm some people. Also, the right to carry a firearm may be restricted on private property and businesses by the owners. Be attentive for signs warning of restricted areas when carrying firearms into public places. If approached by law enforcement for official business such as traffic stops or complaint related inquiries, it is recommended that you tell the officer in a non-threatening manner that you are carrying a weapon or have a weapon in the vehicle and that you have a valid permit. A law enforcement officer does have the right to inspect the permit.

**Employee Carry:** In Indiana a business owner cannot enforce any policy that prohibits or has the effect of prohibiting; an employee of the person, including a contract employee, from possessing a firearm or ammunition that is locked in the trunk of the employee's vehicle, kept in the glove compartment of the employee's locked vehicle, or stored out of plain sight in the employee's locked vehicle. (Ind. Code §34-28-7)

**DNR Property:** The prohibition against DNR property **does not apply to permit holders**, however the prohibition against Army Corp property and Falls of the Ohio State Park still apply. **For those without a permit**, uncased firearms are also not permitted in the following DNR properties: (1) Nature preserves, (2) state museums and historic sites, (3) Campgrounds, (4) Picnic areas, (5) Beaches, (6) Service areas, (7) Headquarters buildings, (8) Hunter check stations, (9) Developed recreation sites. (312 Ind. Admin. Code 8-2-3(b))

**School Parking Lots:** The prohibition against firearms on school property does not apply to the following:

- A person who: (A) may legally possess a firearm; and (B) possesses the firearm in a motor vehicle that is being operated by the person to transport another person to or from a school or a school function.

- A person who: (A) may legally possess a firearm; and (B) possesses a firearm that is: (i) locked in the trunk of the person's motor vehicle; (ii) kept in the glove compartment of the person's locked motor vehicle; or (iii) stored out of plain sight in the person's locked motor vehicle.

## Iowa

*"The Iowa Constitution contains NO provision for the right to keep and bear arms."*

**Rating:** ★ ★ ★ ★

State of Iowa
Office of the Attorney General
Hoover State Office Building
1305 East Walnut
Des Moines, IA 50319

## Prohibited Areas

**Places Off Limits to Firearms Under State Law:**

1. Real property of a public park (Iowa Code §724.4A(1))

2. Public and private school (within 1000 feet) or school buses. (Iowa Code §724.4A(1))

3. Casino (without express written permission) (Iowa Code §491-5.4(6))

4. State buildings on the Capitol Complex (Iowa Code §11-100.2(8a))

   a. Effective 4-17-17 this law only applies to open carry and does not prohibit concealed carry by permit holders.

5. State Fair Grounds (Iowa Code §371-2.5)

6. University Property (Iowa Admin Code r. 681-9.1(262))

7. City and County property if posted (AG opinion No. 03-4-1)

8. Courthouses: All weapons are prohibited from courtrooms, court-controlled spaces, and public areas of courthouses and other justice centers occupied by the court system. (June 19, 2017 Iowa Supreme Court Order, Iowa Code §724.32)

**Permits Recognized By This State:** ALL STATE PERMITS.

### Special Notes:

**Weapons free zones**—enhanced penalties. (**Legal Heat note:** The wording of this section is very ambiguous. Although we believe this section simply institutes a harsher penalty for the commission of public offenses within a "weapons free zone" it could be argued that it also prohibits the mere carrying of a firearm in these areas, as it gives no exceptions for permit holders. (Iowa Code §724.4)

- *As used in this section, "weapons free zone" means the area in or on, or within one thousand feet of, the real property comprising a public or private elementary or secondary school, or in or on the real property comprising a public park. A weapons free zone shall not include that portion of a public park designated as a hunting area under (Iowa Code §461A.42)*

## Police Encounter - Quasi Duty To Inform:

Iowa is a *quasi duty to inform* state, which means that you are not affirmatively required to tell a police officer that you have a firearm in your possession, but if you are asked by an officer during a lawful stop you must provide them with your permit.

- **The Law:** A person armed with a revolver, pistol, or pocket billy concealed upon the person shall have in the person's immediate possession the permit and shall produce the permit for inspection at the request of a peace officer. Failure to so produce a permit is a simple misdemeanor. Iowa Code Ann. § 724.5

**State Parks:** *"The Department's position on **state parks, preserves, and refuges** is as follows: A person with a valid permit may carry their firearm; however **the use of that firearm is prohibited**. Use would be brandishing, displaying, bartering, striking with, and, most obviously, firing or attempting to fire the weapon."* [http://bit.ly/llstgH]

**Alcohol Prohibited:** A permit issued under this chapter is invalid if the person to whom the permit is issued is intoxicated. (Iowa Code §724.4C). In Iowa, "intoxicated" means having an alcohol concentration of .08 or more. (Iowa Code 321J.2)

**University Property:** The universities are authorized to adopt other definitions of misconduct in addition to those in this rule. Any person, student, member of the faculty or staff, or visitor, who intentionally commits, attempts to commit, or incites or aids others in committing any of the following acts shall be subject to disciplinary action ... Use or possession on the campus or at or during any university-authorized function or event of firearms, ammunition, or other dangerous weapons, substances, or materials (except as expressly authorized by the university), or of bombs, explosives, or explosive or incendiary devices prohibited by law. Iowa Admin. Code r. 681-9.1(262)

- **Tasers on College/University Property:** A taser or stun gun that fires a projectile is prohibited on university/college property. However, a taser may be carried on campus as long as the taser does not generate a projectile that directs an electric current, impulse, wave, or beam that produces a high-voltage pulse designed to immobilize a person, and it is not used in the commission of a public offense. Iowa Code Ann. § 260C.14A

## Kansas

*"A person has the right to keep and bear arms for the defense of self, family, home and state, for lawful hunting and recreational use, and for any other lawful purpose; but standing armies, in time of peace, are dangerous to liberty, and shall not be tolerated, and the military shall be in strict subordination to the civil power."*

(Bill of Rights,§ 4)

State of Kansas
Office of the Attorney General
120 SW 10th Avenue, 2nd Floor
Topeka, KS 66612

**Rating:** ★ ★

## Prohibited Areas

**Places Off Limits to Firearms Under State Law:**

1. **Posted public buildings with "adequate security"**

   a. The carrying of a concealed handgun shall not be prohibited in any public area of any state or municipal building unless such public area has adequate security measures to ensure that no weapons are permitted to be carried into such public area and the public area is conspicuously posted with either permanent or temporary signage. Kan. Stat. Ann. § 75-7c20

2. **Secure areas of a corrections facility, a jail facility or a law enforcement agency.**

3. **Kansas state school for the deaf or the Kansas state school for the blind.**

4. A state or municipal-owned **medical care facility**, as defined in K.S.A. 65-425.

5. **A community mental health center** organized pursuant to K.S.A.19-4001

6. **Public or Private K-12 school buildings if posted** (K-12 schools do not require "adequate security" to prohibit carry).

7. **Posted businesses and other buildings:** Any person who carries into a posted building without *adequate security* (other than a school) shall not be subject to a criminal penalty but may be subject to denial to such premises or removal from such premises. KS LEGIS 134 (2014), 2014 Kansas Laws Ch. 134 (H.B. 2140).

8. **Race tracks:** (K.A.R. 112-11-21). This prohibition may be preempted by H.B. 2052, but it is still on the books and will be listed here until it is removed from the Kansas Administrative Regulations.

9. **Courtrooms:** The chief judge can prohibit the carrying of concealed firearms into courtrooms provided adequate security is in place. HB 2502, 2016

**Permits Recognized By This State:** **ALL STATE PERMITS.** (Kan. Stat. Ann. §75-7c03)

**Special Notes:**

**Constitutional Carry:** On 07-01-15 Kansas adopted "Constitutional Carry", which means a permit is no longer required to carry a concealed firearm in Kansas so long as the individual is over the age of 21 and is not prohibited from possessing a firearm under state or federal law. (see KS ST 21-6309(d)(4))

**Public Buildings:** In 2013 the Kansas Legislature passed H.B. 2052 which prohibited public buildings from restricting licensed carry of firearms unless "*adequate security measures had been taken*". *Adequate security measures are defined as, "the use of electronic equipment and personnel at public entrances to detect and restrict the carrying of any weapons into the state or municipal building, including, but not limited to, metal detectors, metal detector wands or any other equipment used for similar purposes to ensure that weapons are not permitted to be carried into such building by members of the public. Adequate security measures for storing and securing lawfully carried weapons, including, but not limited to, the use of gun lockers or other similar storage options may be provided at public entrances.*" Legal Heat suggests using caution when attempting to carry into any posted public building until the issue is clarified further. See: FIREARMS —PERSONAL AND FAMILY PROTECTION ACT, 2013 Kansas Laws Ch. 105 (H.B. 2052)

- **State Capitol**: The provisions of this section shall not apply to the carrying of a concealed handgun in the state capitol. An individual may carry a concealed handgun in the state capitol, provided such individual is not prohibited from possessing a firearm under either federal or state law. Kan. Stat. Ann. § 75-7c21

**State and Municipal Employees:** No state agency or municipality shall prohibit an employee who is licensed to carry a concealed handgun under the provisions of the personal and family protection act from carrying such concealed handgun at the employee's work place unless the building has adequate security measures and the building is conspicuously posted in accordance with K.S.A. 75–7c10.

**Adequate Security:** Means the use of electronic equipment and armed personnel at public entrances to detect and restrict the carrying of any weapons into the state or municipal building, or any public area thereof, including, but not limited to, metal detectors, metal detector wands or any other equipment used for similar purposes to ensure that weapons are not permitted to be carried into such building or public area by members of the public.

# Kentucky

*"All men are, by nature, free and equal, and have certain inherent and inalienable rights, among which may be reckoned: ...The right to bear arms in defense of themselves and of the State, subject to the power of the General Assembly to enact laws to prevent persons from carrying concealed weapons."*

§ 1

**Rating:** ★ ★ ★ ★

Kentucky State Police
Legal Office
919 Versailles Road
Frankfort, KY 40601
(502) 695-6318

## Prohibited Areas

### Places Off Limits to Firearms Under State Law:

1. Police station or sheriff's office (Ky. Rev. Stat. Ann. §237.110(16))
2. Detention facility, prison or jail (Ky. Rev. Stat. Ann. §237.110(16))
3. Courthouse (Court of Justice, courtroom or court proceeding) (Ky. Rev. Stat. Ann. §237.110(16))
4. County, municipal, or special district governing body meetings (Ky. Rev. Stat. Ann. §237.110(16))
5. Meeting of governing body of a county, municipality, or special district (Ky. Rev. Stat. Ann. §237.110(16))
6. General Assembly session, including committee meetings (Ky. Rev. Stat. Ann. §237.110(16))
7. Any portion of an establishment licensed to dispense beer or alcoholic beverages for consumption on the premises, which portion of the establishment is primarily devoted to that purpose. (Ky. Rev. Stat. Ann. §237.110(16)). (does not apply to restaurants that are open to the public, have dining facilities for at least 50 people, and receive at least 50 percent of their gross annual income from the sale of food. (Ky. Rev. Stat. Ann. § 244.125))
8. Elementary or secondary school facilities (without the consent of school authorities). (Ky. Rev. Stat. Ann. §237.110(16))
   a. This prohibition does not apply to an adult who is not a pupil of any secondary school and who possesses a firearm, if the firearm is contained within a vehicle operated by the adult and is not removed from the vehicle, except for a purpose permitted herein, or brandished by the adult, or by any other person acting with expressed or implied consent of the adult, while the vehicle is on school property; Ky. Rev. Stat. Ann. § 527.070

9. Child-caring facilities, day care centers, or any certified family child care home. (Ky. Rev. Stat. Ann. §237.110(16))

10. Areas within an airport where restricted access is controlled by the inspection of persons or property

11. In addition to the above restrictions, units of state and local governments and postsecondary education facilities (colleges, universities, and technical schools) have the authority to limit the carrying of concealed weapons on property owned or controlled by them, except in glove boxes. (Ky. Rev. Stat. Ann. §237.110(16))

    a. *Mitchell v. University of Kentucky* forbids a university from prohibiting the possession of guns in the glove compartment of a vehicle.

12. Any private business if prohibited by the owner, manager or employer. (Ky. Rev. Stat. Ann. §237.110(17)). If the license holder is an employee of the business, he or she may be subject to disciplinary measures by his or her employer. (Ky. Rev. Stat. Ann. §237.110(17))

13. Kentucky State Fair Board property. (Ky. Rev. Stat. Ann. §247.145)

14. Land between the lakes national recreation area and TVA property (except during hunting season).

**Permits Recognized By This State: ALL STATE PERMITS**

## Special Notes:

**Other Prohibitions:** The owner, business or commercial lessee, or manager of a private business enterprise, day-care center as defined in Ky. Rev. Stat. Ann. §199.894 or certified or licensed family child-care home as defined in Ky. Rev. Stat. Ann. §199.8982, or a health-care facility licensed under KRS Chapter 216B, except facilities renting or leasing housing, may prohibit persons holding concealed deadly weapon licenses from carrying concealed deadly weapons on the premises and may prohibit employees, not authorized by the employer, holding concealed deadly weapons licenses from carrying concealed deadly weapons on the property of the employer. If the building or the premises are open to the public, the employer or business enterprise shall post signs on or about the premises if carrying concealed weapons is prohibited. (Ky. Rev. Stat. Ann. §237.110)

**Vehicle Carry:** An individual may carry a loaded or unloaded firearm in an enclosed compartment originally installed by the manufacturer in a motor vehicle. The firearm will not be considered a concealed firearm under state law and the occupant will not need a concealed carry permit to transport a firearm in this manner. (Ky. Rev. Stat. Ann. §527.020(8))

**Employee Parking:** Employees have a right to store weapons in their vehicle while parked on the property. The US District Ct Eastern District of KentuckyNorthern Division Ashland ruled that an employer can create rules informing employees to keep stored guns concealed in their vehicle.

# Louisiana

*"The right of each citizen to acquire, keep, possess, transport, carry, transfer, and use arms for defense of life and liberty, and for all other legitimate purposes is fundamental and shall not be denied or infringed, and any restriction on this right shall be subject to strict scrutiny.."*

Art. I, § 11

Louisiana State Police
Concealed Handgun Permit Section
P.O. Box 666375
Baton Rouge, LA 70896
(225) 925-4867

**Rating:** ★ ★ ★

## Prohibited Areas

### Places Off Limits to Firearms Under State Law:

No concealed handgun may be carried into and no concealed handgun permit issued shall authorize or entitle a permittee to carry a concealed handgun in any of the following:

1.  A law enforcement office, station, or building.

2.  A detention facility, prison, or jail.

3.  A courthouse or courtroom, provided that a judge may carry such a weapon in his own courtroom.

4.  A polling place.

5.  A meeting place of the governing authority of a political subdivision.

6.  The state capitol building.

7.  Any portion of an airport facility where the carrying of firearms is prohibited under federal law, except that no person shall be prohibited from carrying any legal firearm into the terminal, if the firearm is encased for shipment, for the purpose of checking such firearm as lawful baggage.

8.  Any church, synagogue, mosque, or other similar place of worship, eligible for qualification as a tax-exempt organization under 26 U.S.C. 501, except as provided for in Subsection U (see special note below).

9.  A parade or demonstration for which a permit is issued by a governmental entity.

10. Any *portion* of the permitted area of an establishment that has been granted a Class A-General retail permit, as defined in Part II of Chapter 1 or Part II of Chapter 2 of Title 26 of the Louisiana Revised Statutes of 1950, to sell alcoholic beverages for consumption on the premises.

11. Any school, school campus, or school bus as defined in R.S. 14:95.6.

La. Stat. Ann. § 40:1379.3

**Permits Recognized By This State:** Alabama, Alaska, Arizona, Arkansas, Colorado, Florida, Georgia, Idaho, Indiana, Iowa, Kansas, Kentucky, Maine, Michigan, Minnesota, Mississippi, Missouri, Montana, Nebraska, Nevada, New Hampshire, North Carolina, North Dakota, Ohio, Oklahoma, Pennsylvania, South Carolina, South Dakota, Tennessee, Texas, Utah, Washington, West Virginia, Wisconsin, Wyoming

## Special Notes:

**Duty to Inform:** When any peace officer approaches a permittee in an official manner or with an identified purpose, the permittee shall: 1: Notify the officer that he has a weapon on his person, 2: Submit to a pat down, 3: Allow the officer to temporarily disarm him. (La. Rev. Stat. Ann. §40:1379.3(L), also La. Rev. Stat. Ann.  40:1379.3)

**Exception to Place of Worship Prohibition:** Places of worship may allow congregants to carry firearms so long as they are authorized by the person who has authority over the administration of the church, synagogue, mosque, or other similar place of worship. In 2020 HB334 repealed the requirement for permit holders to undergo an additional 8 hours of training to carry in places of worship. La. Stat. Ann. § 40:1379.3

**Employee Parking Lots:** SB 51 from 2008 restricts an employer from prohibiting the storage of firearms in a parking lot so long as they are kept within a locked container unless the employer provides a secure parking facility that is inaccessible to the public.

**Alcohol:** No individual to whom a concealed handgun permit is issued may carry and conceal such handgun while under the influence of alcohol or a controlled dangerous substance. While a permittee is under the influence of alcohol or a controlled dangerous substance, an otherwise lawful permit is considered automatically suspended and is not valid. A permittee shall be considered under the influence as evidenced by a blood alcohol reading of .05 percent or greater by weight of alcohol in the blood, or when a blood test or urine test shows any confirmed presence of a controlled dangerous substance as defined in R.S. 40:961 and 964. La. Rev. Stat. Ann.  40:1379.3

# Maine

*"Every citizen has a right to keep and bear arms and*

*this right shall never be questioned."*

Art. I, § 16

**Rating: ★ ★ ★**

Department of Public Safety
Maine State Police
Special Services Unit
164 State House Station
Augusta, ME 04333
(207) 624-7068

## Prohibited Areas

**Places Off Limits to Firearms Under State Law:**

1. A person is guilty of criminal possession of a firearm if the person possesses any firearm on the premises of a licensed liquor establishment posted to prohibit or restrict the possession of firearms in a manner reasonably likely to come to the attention of patrons (Me. Rev. Stat. tit.17-A §1057)

2. A person may not possess a firearm on public or private school property or discharge a firearm within 500 feet of school property. (Me. Rev. Stat. tit. 20-A. §6552)

3. Colleges aren't prohibited places by statute, but statute gives colleges authority to prohibit firearms. (Me. Rev. Stat. tit. 20-A, §10009)

4. It is a crime for any person, including, but not limited to, security guards and persons involved in a labor dispute or strike, to be armed with a dangerous weapon, at the site of a labor dispute or strike. (Me. Rev. Stat. tit.20-A §6552)

5. All persons are prohibited from entering any court facility, including any courtroom, or any other area or building within the control or supervision of the Maine Judicial Branch, if armed with a firearm, other dangerous weapon or while in possession of a disabling chemical. (Me. Rev. Stat. tit. 17-A, §1058)

6. Baxter State Park (excluding licensed hunters)

7. Capitol Area Buildings (Me. Code R. 16-219, Ch. 41, § 2)

8. Posted Buildings (Me. Rev. Stat. tit. 17-A, § 402)

9. Licensed Slot Machine Facility (Casino) (Me. Code R. 16-633, Ch. 16, § 1)

**Permits Recognized By This State:** Alaska, Alabama, Arkansas, Arizona, Delaware, Florida, Georgia, Idaho, Indiana, Iowa, Kansas, Kentucky, Louisiana, Michigan, Missouri, New Hampshire, Nebraska, North Carolina, North Dakota, Mississippi, Ohio, Oklahoma, South Dakota, Tennessee, Utah, Virginia, Wyoming

**MAINE HONORS PERMITS FROM ALL STATES THAT HONOR THE MAINE PERMIT, SO LONG AS THEY ARE HELD BY RESIDENTS OF THE STATE THAT ISSUED THE PERMIT. MEANING, IF YOU HAVE A PERMIT FROM YOUR HOME STATE, AND YOUR HOME STATE HONORS MAINE, YOU CAN CARRY IN MAINE. (See 25 MRSA § 2001-A, Sub-§2(F)).**

## Special Notes:

**Constitutional Carry:** On 07-09-15 Maine enacted a Constitutional Carry law, which means that effective October 15, 2015 anyone over the age of 21 may now carry a concealed firearm in Maine without a permit so long as they are otherwise not prohibited from possessing a firearm. See Me. Rev. Stat. tit. 25, § 2001-A-1

**Vehicle Carry:** A person may not, while in or on a motor vehicle or in or on a trailer or other type of vehicle being hauled by a motor vehicle, have a cocked and armed crossbow or a firearm with a cartridge or shell in the chamber or in an attached magazine, clip or cylinder or a muzzle-loading firearm charged with powder, lead and a primed ignition device or mechanism, **except that a person is not otherwise prohibited from possessing a firearm may have in or on a motor vehicle or trailer or other type of vehicle a loaded pistol or revolver.** Me. Rev. Stat. tit. 12, § 11212-1-B

**Police Encounters - Quasi Duty to Inform:** Maine is a **quasi duty to inform** state, which means that you are not affirmatively required to tell a police officer that you have a firearm in your possession, but if you are asked by an officer during a lawful stop you must provide them with your permit.

- **The Law**: Every permit holder, including a nonresident who holds a permit issued by the nonresident's state of residence, shall have the holder's permit in the holder's immediate possession at all times when carrying a concealed handgun and shall display the same on demand of any law enforcement officer. 25 MRSA §2003, sub-§11

**Labor Disputes:** It is a Class D crime for any person, including, but not limited to, security guards and persons involved in a labor dispute or strike, to be armed with a dangerous weapon, as defined in Title 17-A, section 2, subsection 9, at the site of a labor dispute or strike. A person holding a valid permit to carry a concealed firearm is not exempt from this subsection. A security guard is exempt from this subsection to the extent that federal laws, rules or regulations require the security guard to be armed with a dangerous weapon at the site of a labor dispute or strike.

**Parking Lots:** An employer cannot restrict an employee from keeping a firearm in one's vehicle provided the gun is concealed and the vehicle is locked. (26 MRSA §600)

# Maryland

*The Maryland Constitution contains NO provision for the right to keep and bear arms.*

**Rating:** ★

Maryland State Police
1201 Reisterstown Road
Pikesville, MD 21208
(410) 486-3101

## Prohibited Areas

**Places Off Limits to Firearms Under State Law:**

1. Public school property (Md. Code Ann. Crim. Law §4-102)

2. A person may not have a firearm in the person's possession or on or about the person at a demonstration in a public place or in a vehicle that is within 1,000 feet of a demonstration in a public place after: (i) the person has been advised by a law enforcement officer that a demonstration is occurring at the public place; and (ii) the person has been ordered by the law enforcement officer to leave the area of the demonstration until the person disposes of the firearm. (Md. Code Ann. Crim. Law §4-208)

3. A person may not willfully bring an assault weapon or other firearm or destructive device...into or have an assault weapon or other firearm or destructive device in a building where (Md. Code Ann. Crim. Law §2-1702):

    a. The Senate or the House has a chamber;

    b. A member, officer, or employee of the General Assembly has an official office; or

    c. A committee of the General Assembly, the Senate, or the House has an office.

4. Chesapeake Forest Lands (except when legally hunting, target shooting, or unloaded and encased). (Md. Code Regs. 08.01.07.14)

5. Localities may regulate the carrying of firearms within 100 yards of or in:

    a. A park

    b. A church

    c. A school

    d. A public building

    e. Any other place of public assembly.

       (Md. Code Ann. Crim. Law §4-209(b)(1))

**Permits Recognized By This State: NONE**

## Special Notes:

**Large Capacity Magazine:** Maryland defines a large capacity magazine as one that contains 10+ rounds.  The sale, purchase, or transfer of large capacity magazines is banned

**Permit to Purchase:** In Maryland you are required to take a firearm safety training prior to purchasing a firearm. The safety training is defined as general instruction regarding safety in the use and storage of firearms, required for purchase or acquisition of handguns and other regulated firearms after January 1, 2002

**Storage of Firearms:** It is unlawful for any person to store or leave a loaded firearm in any location where the individual knew or should have known that an unsupervised person under the age of sixteen would gain access to the firearm. (Md. Code Ann. Crim Law §4-104)

**Hunting:** You may not carry a firearm while bow hunting. Nat. Resource 10-408

**Wollard v. Sheridan:** A recent Maryland District Court case (Wollard v. Sheridan) ruled that Maryland's requirement that applicants for a concealed carry permit show  "good and substantial reason to wear, carry, or transport a handgun" is unconstitutional. The case was appealed to the Fourth Circuit Court of Appeals, which issued a temporary stay on the District Court's ruling before overturning the lower court. In a crushing defeat to gun rights in Maryland, the case was subsequently denied certiorari by the U.S. Supreme Court.

# Massachusetts

*"The people have a right to keep and to bear arms for the common defense. And as, in time of peace, armies are dangerous to liberty, they ought not to be maintained without the consent of the legislature; and the military power shall always be held in an exact subordination to the civil authority, and be governed by it."*

*Pt. 1, art. 17*

**Rating: ★ ★**

Massachusetts State Police
Firearms Record Bureau
Criminal History Systems Board
200 Arlington Street, Suite 2200
Chelsea, MA 02150
(617) 660-4600

## Prohibited Areas

### Places Off Limits to Firearms Under State Law:

1. In any building or on the grounds of any elementary or secondary school, college or university (without the written authorization of the board or officer in charge of the elementary or secondary school, college or university). Mass. Gen. Laws Ann. ch. 269, § 10.

2. Posted Buildings. Mass. Gen. Laws Ann. ch. 266, § 120

3. Public activities in nature preserves. 321 CMR 11.07(15)

4. In or within watersheds and watershed systems. 350 CMR 11.09(21)

5. Courthouses

**Permits Recognized By This State: NONE**

## Special notes:

**H.4376:** On 08-13-14 Governor Patrick signed H.4376 (AKA the Acts of 2014 - Chapter 284). Several changes were made including adding harsher penalties associated with possessing a firearm on school grounds, expanding the eligibility disqualifications for firearm identification cards and licenses to carry, and the implementation of the web portal through which all personal sales/transfers of firearms must be completed. Most of the law changes, however, do not affect the content of the Legal Heat book.

**Large Capacity Magazine:** Massachusetts defines large capacity as a magazine that can hold 10+ rounds. Sale, transfer, or possession is prohibited. (Mass. Gen Laws ch. 140, §121.)

**Police Encounters - Quasi Duty To Inform:** Massachusetts is a quasi duty to inform state, which means that you are not affirmatively required to tell a police officer that you have a firearm in your possession, but if you are asked by an officer during a lawful stop you must provide them with your permit.

- **The Law:** Any person who, while not being within the limits of his own property or residence, or such person whose property or residence is under lawful search, and who is not exempt under this section, **shall on demand of a police officer or other law enforcement officer, exhibit his license to carry firearms, or his firearm identification card** or receipt for fee paid for such card...Upon failure to do so such person may be required to surrender to such officer said firearm, rifle or shotgun which shall be taken into custody as under the provisions of section one hundred and twenty-nine D, except that such firearm, rifle or shotgun shall be returned forthwith upon presentation within thirty days of said license to carry firearms, firearm identification card or receipt for fee paid for such card or hunting license as hereinbefore described. Any person subject to the conditions of this paragraph may, even though no firearm, rifle or shotgun was surrendered, be required to produce within thirty days said license to carry firearms, firearm identification card or receipt for fee paid for such card, or said hunting license, failing which the conditions of section one hundred and twenty-nine D will apply. Nothing in this section shall prevent any person from being prosecuted for any violation of this chapter.
Mass. Gen. Laws Ann. ch. 140, § 129C

**Storage of a Firearm:** It shall be unlawful to store or keep any firearm, rifle or shotgun including, but not limited to, large capacity weapons, or machine gun in any place unless such weapon is secured in a locked container or equipped with a tamper-resistant mechanical lock or other safety device, properly engaged so as to render such weapon inoperable by any person other than the owner or other lawfully authorized user. (Mass. Gen Laws. ch.140 §131L(a))

**OHVs:** The Massachusetts Department of Conservation and Recreation guidelines prohibit the carrying of firearms on off highway vehicles unless unloaded and encased.

**Mount Greylock State Preservation:** No Hunting or firearms are permitted within the War Memorial Park, a 0.75-mile radius from the War Memorial Tower. Target shooting or target practice is prohibited. (See Mass DCR Regulations, 304 Mass. Code Regs. 17.00-17.08)

**Woods Hole, Martha's Vineyard and Nantucket Steamship Authority:** If you're planning on utilizing one of these, you may transport firearms if you have a permit. However, there are certain conditions that must be met. Consult the relevant authority, or check their Customer Handbook, section J 2.1.

# Michigan

*"Every person has a right to keep and bear arms for*

*the defense of himself and the state."*

*Art. I, § 6*

**Rating:** ★ ★ ★

Michigan State Police
Firearms Record Unit
7150 Harris Dr.
Lansing, MI 48913

## Prohibited Areas

**Places Off Limits to Firearms Under State Law:**

An individual licensed to carry a concealed pistol shall not carry a concealed pistol on the premises of any of the following:

1.  A school or school property except that a parent or legal guardian of a student of the school is not precluded from carrying a concealed pistol while in a vehicle on school property, if he or she is dropping the student off at the school or picking up the student from the school. As used in this section, "school" and "school property" mean those terms as defined in section 237a of the Michigan penal code, 1931 PA 328, MCL 750.237a.

2.  A public or private child care center or day care center, public or private child caring institution, or public or private child placing agency. Mich. Comp. Laws Ann. § 28.425o

3.  A sports arena or stadium. Mich. Comp. Laws Ann. § 28.425o

4.  A bar or tavern licensed under the Michigan liquor control code where the primary source of income of the business is the sale of alcoholic liquor by the glass and consumed on the premises. Mich. Comp. Laws Ann. § 28.425o

    a.  This section does not apply to an owner or employee of the business. The Michigan liquor control commission shall develop and make available to holders of licenses under the Michigan liquor control code an appropriate sign stating that "This establishment prohibits patrons from carrying concealed weapons".

5.  Any property or facility owned or operated by a church, synagogue, mosque, temple, or other place of worship, unless the presiding official or officials of the church, synagogue, mosque, temple, or other place of worship permit the carrying of concealed pistol on that property or facility. Mich. Comp. Laws Ann. § 28.425o

6.  An entertainment facility with a seating capacity of 2,500 or more individuals that the individual knows or should know has a seating capacity of 2,500 or more individuals or that has a sign above each public entrance stating in letters not less than 1-inch high a seating capacity of 2,500 or more individuals. Mich. Comp. Laws Ann. § 28.425o

7.  A hospital. Mich. Comp. Laws Ann. § 28.425o

8.  A dormitory or classroom of a community college, college, or university. Mich. Comp. Laws Ann. § 28.425o

9. Casinos. Mich. Admin. Code r. 432.1212

10. Weapons are not permitted in any courtroom, office, or other space used for official court business or by judicial employees unless the chief judge or other person designated by the chief judge has given prior approval. Supreme Court Administrative Order 2001-1

**Permits Recognized By This State: ALL STATE PERMITS (Michigan only honors a permit if it is held by a resident of the state that issued the permit)**

## Special Notes:

**State Parks:** There has been some debate as to whether a permit holder may carry a firearm into a state park. The answer is that a permit holder CAN carry into a state park and the Department of Natural Resources is prohibited from promulgating any rule restricting the carry of firearms by permit holders department. Mich. Comp. Laws Ann. § 324.504

**Police Encounters - Duty to Inform:** In Michigan a licensee who is stopped by a police officer in Michigan is required to immediately inform the peace officer that he or she is carrying a firearm as well as have their license to carry in their immediate possession at all times.

- **The Law:** An individual licensed under this act to carry a concealed pistol and who is carrying a concealed pistol or a portable device that uses electro-muscular disruption technology and who is stopped by a peace officer shall immediately disclose to the peace officer that he or she is carrying a pistol or a portable device that uses electro-muscular disruption technology concealed upon his or her person or in his or her vehicle. Mich. Comp. Laws Ann. § 28.425f (3)

**Non-Resident Permits:** Michigan is a "Resident Only State" which means that although they recognize all other state's permits, they only recognize these permits if they are held by a resident of that state (ie. a Florida resident holding a Florida permit).

**Open Carry At Polling Places:** On 10/16/20 Michigan Secretary of State Jocelyn Benson issued a directive prohibiting the open carry of firearms within 100 feet of a polling place, clerk's office(s), or absent voter counting board:

- **The Directive:** "The open carry of a firearm is prohibited in a polling place, in any hallway used by voters to enter or exit, or within 100 feet of any entrance to a building in which a polling place is located. A person may leave a firearm inside a vehicle parked within 100 feet of the building when visiting these locations if otherwise permitted by law to possess the firearm within the vehicle."

**Alcohol:** An individual carrying a concealed pistol with any BAC is subject to immediate seizure of their pistol and the following penalties:

- BAC of .02 - .07 = State civil infraction, $100 fine, and up to 1-year CPL license revocation.
- BAC of .08 - .09 = 93-day misdemeanor, $100 fine, and up to 3-year CPL license revocation.
- BAC of .10 or more = 93-day misdemeanor, $100 fine, and permanent CPL license revocation.

**Vehicle Carry**: No carry in a vehicle without a permit

- A person shall not carry a pistol concealed on or about his or her person, or, whether concealed or otherwise, in a vehicle operated or occupied by the person, except in his or her dwelling house, place of business, or on other land possessed by the person, without a license to carry the pistol as provided by law and if licensed, shall not carry the pistol in a place or manner inconsistent with any restrictions upon such license. Mich. Comp. Laws Ann. § 750.227

- A person licensed to carry a concealed pistol may lawfully occupy a motor vehicle in which a pistol has been left that belongs to another person who has exited the vehicle. 2003 Mich. Op. Atty. Gen. No. 7136, 2003 WL 21796196 (Mich. A.G. July 30, 2003)

- A person who is not licensed to carry a concealed pistol may lawfully occupy a vehicle in which a pistol has been left that is lawfully contained and that belongs to another person who has exited the vehicle, only if the occupant is not carrying the weapon, a determination that depends on the facts of each case. 2003 Mich. Op. Atty. Gen. No. 7136, 2003 WL 21796196 (Mich. A.G. July 30, 2003)

# Minnesota

*The Minnesota Constitution contains NO provision for the right to keep and bear arms.*

**Rating:** ★ ★

State of Minnesota
Office of the Attorney General
State Capitol, Suite 102
St. Paul, MN 55155
(651) 296-6196

## Prohibited Areas

**Places Off Limits to Firearms Under State Law:**

1. Public and private K-12 school property, including busses (Minn. Stat. §609.66(2)(1d))
2. A childcare center while children are present
3. Posted Establishments (including churches): May be verbal or via "no guns" sign. (Minn. Stat. §624.714)
4. Places of employment, public or private, if employer restricts the carry or possession of firearms by is employees
5. A public post secondary institution may establish policies that restrict the carry or possession of firearms by its students while on the institution's property
    a. An employer or a post-secondary institution may not prohibit the lawful carry or possession of firearms in a parking facility or parking area.
6. State correctional facilities or state hospitals and grounds (Minn. Stat. §243.55)
7. Any jail, lockup or correctional facility (Minn. Stat. §641.165)
8. Courthouse complexes, unless the sheriff is notified (Minn. Stat. §609.66)
9. Offices and courtrooms of the Minnesota Supreme Court and Court of Appeals
10. Any state building unless the commissioner of public safety is notified (Minn. Stat. §609.66)
11. In federal court facilities or other federal facilities (Title 18 U.S.C. §930)

**Permits Recognized By This State:** Alaska, Delaware, Idaho (enhanced permit only), Illinois, Kansas, Kentucky, Louisiana, Michigan, New Jersey, New Mexico, North Dakota (class 1 permit only), Rhode Island, South Carolina, South Dakota (enhanced permit only), West Virginia ("regular" permits only).

## Special Notes:

**Permitless Carry:** You do not need a permit in Minnesota to:

- Keep or carry about one's place of business, dwelling, or land
- To carry a pistol from a place of purchase to a dwelling or place of business
- To carry between a dwelling and place of business
- To carry a pistol in the woods or fields or waters for purposes of hunting
- To transport a pistol in a motor vehicle, snowmobile, or boat if the pistol is unloaded and contained in a closed and fastened case. (Minn. Stat. §624.714)

**Churches:** In *Edina Community Lutheran Church v. Minnesota*, Minn. Court of Appeals, A07-131, the court ruled that a church may ban firearms in its buildings and parking areas.

**Police Encounters:** Minnesota is a **quasi duty to inform** state, which means that you are not affirmatively required to tell a police officer that you have a firearm in your possession, but if you are asked by an officer during a lawful stop you must provide them with your permit and photo identification card.

- **The Law:** The holder of a permit to carry must have the permit card and a driver's license, state identification card, or other government-issued photo identification in immediate possession at all times when carrying a pistol and must display the permit card and identification document upon lawful demand by a peace officer. MN ST § 624.714

**Duty to Render Aid to Shooting Victim:** A person who discharges a firearm and knows or should know that the discharge has caused bodily harm to another person must immediately investigate the extent of the injuries and render immediate reasonable assistance to the injured person. A person who violates this duty is subject to criminal penalties that vary according to the extent of the shooting victim's injuries. A person who witnesses a shooting incident is subject to the same duty to investigate and render aid and is also subject to criminal penalties for failing to do so. Minn. Stat. Ann. § 609.662

**Posted Buildings:** A person carrying a firearm on or about his or her person or clothes under a permit or otherwise who remains at a private establishment knowing that the operator of the establishment or its agent has made a reasonable request that firearms not be brought into the establishment may be ordered to leave the premises. A person who fails to leave when so requested is guilty of a petty misdemeanor. MN ST § 624.714

# Mississippi

*"The right of every citizen to keep and bear arms in defense of his home, person, or property, or in aid of the civil power when thereto legally summoned, shall not be called in question, but the legislature may regulate or forbid carrying concealed weapons."*

*Art. III, § 12*

**Rating:** ★ ★ ★

Mississippi Highway Patrol
Gun Permits
P.O. Box 958
Jackson, MS 39205
(601) 987-1212

## Prohibited Areas

**Places Off Limits to Firearms Under State Law:**

1. Any place of nuisance as defined in Miss. Code. Ann. §95-3-1
2. Any police, sheriff or highway patrol station (Miss. Code. Ann. §45-9-101(13))
3. Any detention facility, prison or jail (Miss. Code. Ann. §45-9-101(13))
4. Any courthouse; any courtroom (Miss. Code. Ann. §45-9-101(13))
   a. "Courthouse" means any building in which a circuit court, chancery court, youth court, municipal court, justice court or any appellate court is located, or any building in which a court of law is regularly held.
   b. "Courtroom" means the actual room in which a judicial proceeding occurs, including any jury room, witness room, judge's chamber, office housing the judge's staff, or similar room. "Courtroom" shall not mean hallways, courtroom entrances, courthouse grounds, lobbies, corridors, or other areas within a courthouse which are generally open to the public for the transaction of business outside of an active judicial proceeding, the grassed areas, cultivated flower beds, sidewalks, parking lots, or other areas contained within the boundaries of the public land upon which the courthouse is located. Miss. Code. Ann. § 97-37-7
5. Any polling place; any meeting place of the governing body of any governmental entity (Miss. Code. Ann. §45-9-101(13))
6. Any meeting of the Legislature or a committee thereof (Miss. Code. Ann. §45-9-101(13))
7. Any School, college, or professional athletic event not related to firearms (Miss. Code. Ann. §45-9-101(13))
8. Educational property: includes any public or private school building or bus, public or private school campus, grounds, recreational area, athletic field, or other property owned, used or operated by any local school board, school, college or university board of trustees, or directors for the administration of any public or private educational institution or during a school related activity. (Miss. Code. Ann. §97-37-17(1)(a))
   a. Notwithstanding the foregoing, it is not a violation of section 97-37-17 for a licensee to possess or carry, whether openly or concealed, any

handgun on educational property if: A) The person is not a student attending school on any educational property; B) The firearm is within a motor vehicle; and C) The person does not brandish, exhibit or display the handgun in any careless, angry or threatening manner. (Miss. Code Ann. § 97-37-17(6))

9.  Any portion of an establishment, licensed to dispense alcoholic beverages for consumption on the premises that is primarily devoted to dispensing alcoholic beverages (Miss. Code. Ann. §45-9-101(13))

10. Any portion of an establishment in which beer or light wine is consumed on the premises, that is primarily devoted to such purpose (Miss. Code. Ann. §45-9-101(13))

11. Any elementary or secondary school facility (Miss. Code. Ann. §45-9-101(13))

12. Any junior college, community college, college or university facility (Miss. Code. Ann. §45-9-101(13))

13. Inside the passenger terminal of any airport (Miss. Code. Ann. §45-9-101(13))

14. Any church or other place of worship (Miss. Code. Ann. §45-9-101(13))

15. In addition to the places enumerated in this subsection, the carrying of a concealed pistol or revolver may be disallowed in anyplace in the discretion of the person or entity exercising control over the physical location of such place by the placing of a written notice clearly readable at a distance of not less than ten (10) feet that the "carrying of a pistol or revolver is prohibited."

16. No license issued pursuant to this section shall authorize the participants in a parade or demonstration for which a permit is required to carry a concealed pistol or revolver. (Miss. Code. Ann. §45-9-101(13))

**Permits Recognized By This State:  ALL STATE PERMITS**

## Special Notes:

**Posted Buildings:** Posted buildings are defined in Mississippi as "any place that in the discretion of the person or entity exercising control over the physical location of such place (may be posted) by the placing of a written notice clearly readable at a distance of not less than 10 feet that the carrying firearms is prohibited".

**Enhanced Permit Holders:** As of July 1, 2011, one who voluntarily completes additional firearms training can obtain an enhanced endorsement on their permit, which allows the licensee to carry in courthouses, except in courtrooms during a judicial proceeding, and any location listed in subsection (13) of Section 45-9-101, except any place of nuisance as defined in Section 95-3-1, any police, sheriff or highway patrol station or any detention facility, prison or jail. (Miss. Code. Ann. §97-37-7(2)) The Mississippi Attorney General's office has issued an opinion clarifying where an enhanced permit holder can/cannot carry (AG Opinion dated Dec. 5, 2013). **A person with an enhanced permit may carry in the below areas regardless of signage posted by a state governmental entity:**

1.  Any polling place. − (Other than the Section 45-9-101(13) prohibiting regular permit holders from carrying in polling places, Mississippi Code Sections

23-15-895 (relating to armed candidates) and 97-13-29 (military officer keeping armed troops within one mile of an election) are the only other state law restrictions regarding firearms in polling places.)

2.  Any meeting place of the governing body of any governmental entity. – (It is the opinion of this office that the phrase meeting place means the room in which a meeting transpires as opposed to the entire building. Thus, although an enhanced permit holder would be entitled to carry a concealed pistol or revolver into a meeting place, that individual would not have unfettered gun carrying access to places within the building that are not generally open to the general public. See MS AG Op. Cantrell (Oct. 1, 2013)).

3.  Any meeting of the Legislature or a committee thereof. – (Notwithstanding this language, it is the understanding of this office that the House and the Senate have each passed rules or regulations restricting the right of individuals to carry weapons at meetings of the Legislature or its committees.)

4.  Any school, college or professional athletic event not related to firearms. – (This provision authorizes an enhanced permit holder to carry a stun gun, concealed pistol or revolver into non-firearm related events even if signage is posted pursuant to Section 45-9- 101(13). However, if signage were posted relating to a firearm related school, college or professional event, enhanced permit holders would not be authorized to carry their weapons.)

5.  Any portion of an establishment, licensed to dispense alcoholic beverages for consumption on the premises, that is primarily devoted to dispensing alcoholic beverages. -- (This provision would only have applicability to governmental entities to the extent that such entities owned an establishment that was primarily devoted to consuming alcoholic beverages.)

6.  Any portion of an establishment in which beer or light wine is consumed on the premises, that is primarily devoted to such purpose. -- (This provision would only have applicability to governmental entities to the extent that such entities owned an establishment that was primarily devoted to consuming beer or light wine.)

7.  Any elementary or secondary school facility. – (See MS AG Op. Cantrell (Oct. 1, 2013)).

8.  Any junior college, community college, college or university facility.

9.  Inside the passenger terminal of any airport. – (Any person may bring a weapon into a passenger terminal if brought in for the purposes of properly lawfully checking or shipping such weapon. An enhanced permit holder could of course still be arrested under federal law for possessing a weapon in areas prohibited by federal law.)

10. Any church or other place of worship. (Practically speaking this provision would not apply to public entities who do not own or control places of worship. This provision has little practical value because private land owners can generally always allow or disallow anyone from carrying a weapon on their private property regardless of whether the state has granted a license. – See MS AG Op. Cantrell (Oct. 1, 2013)).

11. Any place where the carrying of firearms is prohibited by federal law. – (This provision can only be read to mean that an enhanced permit holder carrying a weapon on prohibited federal property would not be subject to prosecution

for state law violations. The federal government certainly could and probably would prosecute anyone bringing a weapon into an unauthorized area regardless of the person's possession of a state permit.).

12. In a parade or demonstration for which a permit is required.

13. In courthouses except in courtrooms during a judicial proceeding. -- (The right to carry in courthouses except in courtrooms during judicial proceedings is granted to enhanced permit holders expressly by Section 97-37-7 without reference to Section 45-9- 101(13). Section 45-9-101(13) states that regular permit holders may not carry in "courthouses" or "courtrooms" with the caveat that nothing contained therein precludes a judge from determining who "will" carry a weapon "in his courtroom." Presumably under this authority, a judge has authority to determine who will, who can and who cannot carry a weapon in his courtroom. However, the governing authority of the jurisdiction, whether municipal or county could restrict a regular permit holder from initial entry into the courthouse, as opposed to the courtroom, by posting a sign. However, such signage could not prevent an enhanced permit holder from entry into the courthouse. Under no interpretation of the law would either a regular or enhanced permit holder be authorized to carry a firearm into a courtroom during a judicial proceeding unless authorized by the judge. Likewise, as noted above, an individual would not have unfettered gun carrying access to places within the building that are not generally open to the general public. See MS AG Op. Cantrell (Oct. 1, 2013).

**This opinion does not affect the rights of property owners or custodians as follows:**

1. Private landowners may post signs or otherwise prevent carrying of weapons onto their private property.

2. State or local governmental entities may prohibit concealed carry by enhanced permit holders into areas posted with no weapons signage if the place is not one of the 13 enumerated places above.

3. Federal installations and buildings can prohibit the carrying of weapons regardless of these state statutes.

# Missouri

*"That the right of every citizen to keep and bear arms in defense of his home, person and property, or when lawfully summoned in aid of the civil power, shall not be questioned; but this shall not justify the wearing of concealed weapons."*

*Art. I, § 23*

**Rating:** ★ ★ ★

State of Missouri
Office of the Attorney General
Supreme Court Building
207 West High Street
Jefferson City, MO 65101
(573) 751-3321

## Prohibited Areas

### Places Off Limits to Firearms Under State Law:

A concealed carry endorsement shall not authorize carry into (Mo. Rev. Stat. §571.107):

1.  Any police, sheriff, or highway patrol office or station without the consent of the chief law enforcement officer in charge of that office or station.

2.  Within twenty-five feet of any polling place on any election day.

3.  The facility of any adult or juvenile detention or correctional institution, prison or jail.

4.  Any courthouse solely occupied by the circuit, appellate or supreme court, or any courtrooms, administrative offices, libraries or other rooms of any such court whether or not such court solely occupies the building in question.

5.  Any meeting of the governing body of a unit of local government; or any meeting of the general assembly or a committee of the general assembly, except that nothing in this subdivision shall preclude a member of the body holding a valid concealed carry endorsement from carrying a concealed firearm at a meeting of the body which he or she is a member.

6.  The general assembly, supreme court, county or municipality may by rule, administrative regulation, or ordinance prohibit or limit the carrying of concealed firearms by endorsement holders in that portion of a building owned, leased or controlled by that unit of government. (These areas will be clearly posted)

7. Any establishment licensed to dispense intoxicating liquor for consumption on the premises, which portion is primarily devoted to that purpose, without the consent of the owner or manager. The provisions of this subdivision shall not apply to the licensee of said establishment. The provisions of this subdivision shall not apply to any bona fide restaurant open to the general public having dining facilities for not less than fifty persons and that receives at least fifty-one percent of its gross annual income from the dining facilities by the sale of food

8. Any area of an airport to which access is controlled by the inspection of persons and property.

9. Any place where the carrying of a firearm is prohibited by federal law;

10. Any higher education institution or elementary or secondary school facility without the consent of the governing body of the higher education institution or a school official or the district school board. Possession of a firearm in a vehicle on the premises of any higher education institution or elementary or secondary school facility shall not be a criminal offense so long as the firearm is not removed from the vehicle or brandished while the vehicle is on the premises;

11. Any portion of a building used as a child-care facility without the consent of the manager. Nothing in this subdivision shall prevent the operator of a child-care facility in a family home from owning or possessing a firearm or a driver's license or no driver's license containing a concealed carry endorsement;

12. Any riverboat gambling operation accessible by the public without the consent of the owner or manager pursuant to rules promulgated by the gaming commission.

13. Any gated area of an amusement park;

14. Any church or other place of religious worship without the consent of the minister or person or persons representing the religious organization that exercises control over the place of religious worship;

15. Any private property whose owner has posted the premises as being off-limits to concealed firearms by means of one or more signs displayed in a conspicuous place of a minimum size of eleven inches by fourteen inches with the writing thereon in letters of not less than one inch. An employer may prohibit employees or other persons holding a concealed carry endorsement from carrying a concealed firearm in vehicles owned by the employer;

16. Any sports arena or stadium with a seating capacity of five thousand or more.

17. Any hospital accessible by the public.

18. **Busses:** Any passenger who boards a bus with a dangerous or deadly weapon or other means capable of inflicting serious bodily injury concealed upon his person or effects is guilty of the felony of **"possession and concealment of a dangerous or deadly weapon"** upon a bus. Possession and concealment of a dangerous and deadly weapon by a passenger upon a bus shall be a class C felony. The provisions of this subsection shall not apply to persons who are in possession of weapons or other means of inflicting serious bodily injury with the consent of the owner of such bus, or his agent, or the lessee or bailee of such bus. Mo. Rev. Stat. Ann. § 578.305

**Permits Recognized By This State: ALL STATE PERMITS**

## Special Notes:

**Constitutional Carry:** Effective January 1, 2017 anyone otherwise not prohibited from possessing a firearm may carry a concealed firearm in Missouri without a permit. SB 656, 2016.

# Montana

*"The right of any person to keep or bear arms in defense of his own home, person, and property, or in aid of the civil power when thereto legally summoned, shall not be called in question, but nothing herein contained shall be held to permit the carrying of concealed weapons."*

*Art. II, § 12*

**Rating:** ★ ★ ★ ★

State of Montana
Department of Justice
215 North Sanders
Helena, MT 59260

## Prohibited Areas

**Places Off Limits to Firearms Under State Law:**

1. Portions of a building used for state or local government offices and related areas in the building that have been restricted. (Mont. Code Ann. §45-8-328)

2. A bank, credit union, savings and loan institution, or similar institution during the institution's normal business hours. (Mont. Code Ann. §45-8-328)

3. A room in which alcoholic beverages are sold, dispensed, and consumed under a license issued under Title 16 for the sale of alcoholic beverages for consumption on the premises. (Mont. Code Ann. §45-8-328)

4. Except as authorized by the management of a railroad, it is unlawful for a person not authorized to carry a weapon in the course of his official duties to knowingly or purposely carry or transport firearms on a train in this state unless, prior to boarding, the person has delivered all firearms and ammunition, if any, to the operator of the train. (Mont. Code Ann. §45-8-339)

5. All buildings owned or leased by a local school district that are used for instruction or for student activities. (Mont. Code Ann. §45-8-361)

**Permits Recognized By This State:** Alabama, Alaska, Arizona, Arkansas, California, Colorado, Connecticut, Florida, Georgia, Idaho, Illinois, Indiana, Iowa Kansas, Kentucky, Louisiana, Maryland, Massachusetts, Michigan, Minnesota, Mississippi, Missouri, Nebraska, Nevada, New Jersey, New Mexico, New York, North Carolina, North Dakota, Ohio, Oklahoma, Oregon, Pennsylvania, South Carolina, South Dakota, Tennessee, Texas, Utah, Virginia, Washington, West Virginia, Wisconsin, Wyoming

## Special Notes:

**Poor Preemption - City Prohibitions On Firearms**: Montana has poor state preemption on firearm laws. Montana Code 45-8-351 (2)(a) states "A county, city, town, consolidated local government, or other local government unit has power to prevent and suppress the carrying of concealed or unconcealed firearms to a public assembly, publicly owned building, park under its jurisdiction, or school..." This means in addition to state and federal law, city ordinances may prohibit firearms in a number of additional locations. Although legislation to enact statewide preemption has been proposed, at the time of this publication nothing has been enacted. Accordingly, Legal Heat recommends to check with each city for additional restrictions.

- **Missoula**: City Ordinance 8.58.010 and 8.58.020 prohibit firearms in the following locations: 1. Missoula city hall, 2. Missoula City Council Chambers, 3. City Council meeting buildings, 4. Public museums, 5. Public library, 6. Public parks under the City's jurisdiction, 7. Any public election polling places, 8. Public school building within the city, excluding The University of Montana, 9. Any other locations of public assembly where persons gather together to conduct and/or administer any public election while election related activities are taking place, 10. any public meeting anywhere within the city or public assembly.

**Hotels:** A landlord or operator of a hotel or motel may not, by contract or otherwise, prevent a tenant or a guest of a tenant from possessing on the premises a firearm that it is legal for the tenant or guest to possess. A landlord or operator of a hotel or motel may prohibit the discharge of a firearm on the premises except in self-defense. (Mont. Code Ann. §45-3-103).

**Permitless ("Constitutional") Carry Outside City Limits:** A person does not need a permit to carry a concealed firearm outside the official boundaries of a city or town. (Mont. Code Ann. §45-8-317)

# Nebraska

*"All persons are by nature free and independent, and have certain inherent and inalienable rights; among these are life, liberty, the pursuit of happiness, and the right to keep and bear arms for security or defense of self, family, home, and others, and for lawful common defense, hunting, recreational use, and all other lawful purposes, and such rights shall not be denied or infringed by the state or any subdivision thereof."*

*Art. I, § 1*

**Rating:** ★ ★ ★

Nebraska State Patrol
P.O. Box 94907
Lincoln, NE 68509
(402) 471-4545

## Prohibited Areas

### Places Off Limits to Firearms Under State Law:

1. Police, Sheriff, or Nebraska State Patrol station or office. (272 Neb. Admin. Code Ch.21, §018)

2. Detention facility, prison, or jail. (272 Neb. Admin. Code Ch.21, §018)

3. Courtroom or building which contains a courtroom (272 Neb. Admin. Code Ch.21, §018)

4. Polling place during a bona fide election. (272 Neb. Admin. Code Ch.21, §018)

5. Meeting of the governing body of a county, public school district, municipality, or other political subdivision. (272 Neb. Admin. Code Ch.21, §018)

6. Meeting of the Legislature or a Committee of the Legislature. (272 Neb. Admin. Code Ch.21, §018)

7. Financial Institution. (272 Neb. Admin. Code Ch.21, §018)

8. Professional or semiprofessional athletic event. (272 Neb. Admin. Code Ch.21, §018)

9. Building, grounds, vehicle, or sponsored activity or athletic event of any public, private, denominational, or parochial school or private or public university, college, or community college. (272 Neb. Admin. Code Ch.21, §018)

10. Place of worship. (272 Neb. Admin. Code Ch.21, §018)

11. Hospital, emergency room, or trauma center. (272 Neb. Admin. Code Ch.21, §018)

12. Political rally or fundraiser. (272 Neb. Admin. Code Ch.21, §018)

13. Establishment having a license issued under the Nebraska Liquor Control Act that derives over gone- half of its total income from the sale of alcoholic liquor. (272 Neb. Admin. Code Ch.21, §018)

14. A place or premises where the person, persons, entity, or entities in control of the property or employer in control of the property has prohibited permit holders from carrying concealed handguns into or onto the place or premises. (272 Neb. Admin. Code Ch.21, §018)

15. School grounds or a school-owned vehicle. (272 Neb. Admin. Code Ch.21, §018)

**Permits Recognized By This State:** Alaska, Arizona, Arkansas, California, Colorado, Connecticut, Florida, Hawaii, Idaho (enhanced permit only), Iowa (non-professional only), Illinois, Kansas, Kentucky, Louisiana, Maine, Michigan, Minnesota, Missouri, Montana, Nevada, New Mexico, North Carolina, North Dakota (class 1 & 2), Ohio, Oklahoma, Oregon, South Carolina, South Dakota (Enhanced Permit Only), Tennessee, Texas, Utah, Virginia, West Virginia, Wisconsin, Wyoming (**Only permits issued to someone over the age of 21 are valid in Nebraska**).

## Special Notes:

**Duty to Inform**: Nebraska is a Duty to Inform state, which means when you are stopped by a police officer, or emergency service personnel, you must immediately inform them of the presence of your firearm.

- **The Law**: A permit holder carrying a concealed handgun who is officially contacted by any peace officer or emergency services personnel must immediately inform the peace officer or emergency service personnel of the concealed handgun unless physically unable to do so. (Neb. Rev. Stat. §69-2440(2))

- You must have your permit AND photo ID in your possession while carrying in Nebraska. (Neb. Rev. Stat. §69-2440(1))

**Alcohol**: In Nebraska a permit holder shall not carry a concealed handgun while they are consuming alcohol or have alcohol in his or her blood, urine, or both. (Neb. Rev. Stat. §69-2441)

# Nevada

*"Every citizen has the right to keep and bear arms for security and defense, for lawful hunting and recreational use and for other lawful purposes."*

*Art. I, § 11(1)*

**Rating:** ★ ★ ★

State of Nevada
Office of the Attorney General
Old Supreme Court Building
100 North Carson Street
Carson City, NV 89701
(775) 684-1100

## Prohibited Areas

### Places Off Limits to Firearms Under State Law:

1. Any facility of a law enforcement agency. (Nev. Admin. Code §202.020(1)(A))

2. A prison, city or county jail, or detention facility. (Nev. Admin. Code §202.020(1)(A))

3. Exhibiting or using any firearm or other weapon in a roadside park or safety rest area. (Nev. Admin. Code §408.615(2))

4. A courthouse or courtroom. (Nev. Admin. Code §202.020(1)(A))

5. A public airport and/or a public building that is located on the property of a public airport. (Nev. Rev. Stat. §202.3673)

6. A public building* that has a metal detector at each public entrance or a sign posted at each public entrance indicating that no firearms are allowed in the building. (Nev. Rev. Stat. §202.3673(b))

7. Childcare facility. (Nev. Rev. Stat. §202.265)

8. Any facility of a public or private school without written permission. (Nev. Rev. Stat. §202.3673)

9. Any facility of a vocational/technical school, or the University of Nevada, or Community College System without written permission. (Nev. Rev. Stat. §202.3673)

**Permits Recognized By This State:** Alaska, Arizona, Arkansas, Florida, Idaho (Enhanced Permit Only), Illinois, Kansas, Kentucky, Louisiana, Massachusetts, Michigan, Minnesota, Mississippi (enhanced permit only), Montana, New Mexico, North Carolina, North Dakota (Class I & II permits), Ohio, Oklahoma, Oregon, Rhode Island, South Carolina, South Dakota, Tennessee, Texas, Utah, West Virginia, Wisconsin, Wyoming.

### Special Notes:

**\*Public Building** means any building or office space occupied by: (1) Any component of the Nevada System of Higher Education and used for any purpose related to the System; or  (2) The Federal Government, the State of Nevada or any county, city, school district or other political subdivision of the State of Nevada and used for any public purpose. If only part of the building is occupied by an entity described in this subsection, the term means only that portion of the building, which is so occupied. (Nev. Rev. Stat. §202.3673(6)(b))

**Vehicles:** It is illegal to carry a loaded rifle or shotgun in a vehicle. A rifle or shotgun is loaded when there is an unexpended cartridge in the firing chamber. (Nev. Rev. Stat. §503.165) There is no law against carrying a loaded handgun in a vehicle.

**Statewide Preemption:** With the signing of SB175 on June 3, 2015, Nevada finally gained statewide preemption with regards to concealed carry. Cities (like North Las Vegas) can no longer put in place any regulations regarding the carrying of concealed firearms that exceed the requirements of state law.

**What Guns May You Carry?** Any handgun as defined in 18 U.S.C. §921(a)(29). With the passage of Senate Bill 76 a person may obtain one permit to carry all handguns owned by the person, and such a permit is valid for any handgun with the person owns or thereafter obtains. NRS 202.3657

## New Hampshire

*"All persons have the right to keep and bear arms in defense of themselves, their families, their property and the state."*

*Pt. 1, Art. 2-a*

**Rating:** ★ ★ ★ ★

State of New Hampshire
Department of Public Safety
Division of State Police
Explosives Licenses and Permits Unit
James H. Hayes Safety Building
10 Hazen Drive
Concord, NH 03305
(603) 271-3575

## Prohibited Areas

### Places Off Limits to Firearms Under State Law:

1. Courtrooms (N.H. Rev. Stat. Ann. §159:19)
2. Licensed residential child care facilities (N.H. Code He-C 4001.17),
3. Other licensed childcare facilities (N.H. Code Admin. R. He-C 4002.14),
4. Staffed foster homes (N.H. Code Admin. R. He-C 6446.08),
5. Prison grounds (N.H. Code Admin. R. Cor. 306.01-306.02)
6. Posted buildings. N.H. Rev. Stat. Ann. §635:2
7. The rule adopted by the Facilities Committee stipulates that no one but a law enforcement officer may "carry a firearm or other dangerous or deadly weapon or an explosive, open or concealed," in the State House, the Legislative Office Building and the nearby Upham Walker House. The ban also applies to the underground tunnel connecting the State House and the LOB. Armed law-enforcement officers must produce "sufficient identification" if security staff requests it.

**Permits Recognized By This State:** Alabama, Alaska, Arizona*, Arkansas, Colorado, Florida, Georgia, Idaho, Indiana, Iowa, Kansas, Kentucky, Louisiana, Maine, Michigan Missouri, Mississippi, North Carolina, North Dakota, Ohio, Oklahoma, Pennsylvania, Tennessee, Utah, Virginia, West Virginia, Wyoming (*Must be 21 or older.) (**Resident permits only**)

## Special Notes:

**Constitutional Carry:** Effective 02/22/17 anyone, otherwise not prohibited by New Hampshire law, may carry a concealed firearm in New Hampshire without a permit. N.H. Rev. Stat. Ann. § 159:6

**Storage of Firearms:** Any person who stores or leaves on premises under that person's control a loaded firearm, and who knows or reasonably should know that a child is likely to gain access to the firearm without the permission of the child's parent or guardian, is guilty of a violation if a child gains access to a firearm and (causes harm) (N.H. Rev. Stat. Ann. § 650-C:1)

**Statewide Preemption:** RSA 159:26, which became effective July 2003, details that only the state may regulate firearms, thus cities and states might not be able to enact any additional firearm laws other than discharging restrictions and hunting ordinances.

# New Jersey

*The New Jersey Constitution contains NO provision for the right to keep and bear arms.*

**Rating:** ★

New Jersey State Police
P.O. Box 7068 River Road
West Trenton, NJ 08628
(609) 882-2000

## Prohibited Areas

### Places Off Limits to Firearms Under State Law:

1. In or upon any part of the buildings or grounds of any school, college, university or other educational institution or on any school bus. (N.J. Stat. Ann. §2C:39-5)

2. Casinos, unless you have expressed written permission from Casino Control Commission (N.J. Admin. Code §19:45-1.13)

3. State parks (N.J. Admin. Code §7:2-2.17)

4. Municipalities and counties can independently regulate firearm carry (N.J. Stat. Ann. §40:48-1(18))

## Permits Recognized By This State: NONE

## Special Notes:

**Large Capacity Magazines:** New Jersey prohibits the manufacture, transport, shipment, sale or disposal of large capacity magazines. "Large capacity ammunition magazine" means a box, drum, tube or other container which is capable of holding more than 10 rounds of ammunition to be fed continuously and directly therefrom into a semi-automatic firearm. The term shall not include an attached tubular device which is capable of holding only .22 caliber rimfire ammunition.N.J. Stat. Ann. § 2C:39-1, N.J. Rev. Stat § 2C:39-9h.

**All firearms transported into the State of New Jersey:** Shall be carried unloaded and contained in a closed and fastened case, gun box, securely tied package, or locked in the trunk of the automobile in which it is being transported, and in the course of travel, shall include only such deviations as are reasonably necessary under the circumstances.

The firearm should not be directly accessible from the passenger compartment of the vehicle. If the vehicle does not have a compartment separate from the passenger compartment, the firearm and ammunition must be in a locked container other than the vehicle's glove compartment or console.

**Possession of "Hollow Point" ammunition:** Any person who knowingly has in his possession any hollow nose or dum-dum bullet is guilty of a crime in the fourth degree.

- Exceptions to the hollow point rule include:
  - A person who keeps hollow point ammunition in a dwelling, premises or other land owned or possessed by him, or from carrying such ammunition from the place of purchase to said dwelling or land.
  - A person going directly to an authorized place for "practice, match, target, trap or skeet shooting exhibitions." (N.J. Stat. Ann. §2C:39-3)

**No Preemption:** New Jersey gives its cities and towns the authority to pass ordinances related to firearms. Be mindful cities and towns may have additional restrictions.

## New Mexico

*"No law shall abridge the right of the citizen to keep and bear arms for security and defense, for lawful hunting and recreational use and for other lawful purposes, but nothing herein shall be held to permit the carrying of concealed weapons. No municipality or county shall regulate, in any way, an incident of the right to keep and bear arms."*

*Art. II, § 6*

**Rating:** ★ ★ ★

State of New Mexico
Department of Public Safety
P.O. Box 1628
Santa Fe, NM 87504

## Prohibited Areas

### Places Off Limits to Firearms Under State Law:

1. Liquor establishments that sell hard liquor for consumption on the premises (does not include beer and wine). (N.M. Stat. Ann. §30-7-3)
2. Schools, unless at least 19 years of age and it is in the vehicle (N.M. Stat. Ann. §30-7-2.1)
3. University premises, unless at least 19 years of age and it is in the vehicle (N.M. Stat. Ann. §30-7-2.4)
4. Preschools (N.M. Stat. Ann. §29-19-8)
5. Courts (N.M. Stat. Ann. §29-19-11)
6. Tribal Land (N.M. Stat. Ann. 29-19-10)
7. Public buses (N.M. Stat. Ann. §30-7-13)
8. Game refuge unless crossing etc. (N.M. Stat. Ann. §17-2-12);
9. Jails, prisons, correctional facilities (N.M. Stat. Ann. §30-22-14),
10. Juvenile detention facilities (8.14.1.36, 8.14.5.18);
11. State fairgrounds (4.3.1.19);
12. State monuments if firearm is loaded (4.4.2.17);
13. State library (4.5.7.8);
14. On private property if posted or notified. (10.8.2.16)

**Permits Recognized By This State:** Alaska, Arizona, Arkansas, Colorado, Delaware, Florida, Idaho (Enhanced permit only), Kansas, Michigan, Mississippi, Missouri, Nebraska, Nevada, North Carolina, North Dakota, Ohio, Oklahoma, South Carolina, Tennessee, Texas, Virginia, West Virginia, Wyoming

## Special Notes:

**Vehicle Carry:** A person may carry a loaded firearm (without a permit) in a private automobile or other private means of conveyance, for lawful protection of the person's or another's person or property. N.M. Stat. Ann. § 30-7-2.

**Carry into Alcohol Establishments:** Unlawful carrying of a firearm in an establishment licensed to dispense alcoholic beverages does not include when a **person carrying a concealed handgun who is in possession of a valid concealed handgun license for that gun on the premises of: (a) a licensed establishment that does not sell alcoholic beverages for consumption on the premises**; *or (b) a restaurant licensed to sell only beer and wine that derives no less than sixty percent of its annual gross receipts from the sale of food for consumption on the premises, unless the restaurant has a sign posted, in a conspicuous location at each public entrance, prohibiting the carrying of firearms, or the person is verbally instructed by the owner or manager that the carrying of a firearm is not permitted in the restaurant.* N.M. Stat. Ann. § 30-7-3

**Limit on number of firearms:** Under New Mexico law a permittee may only possess one concealed firearm on or about his or her person at any given time. More firearms may be carried, but not in a concealed manner. These restrictions do not apply to firearms transported or carried in a vehicle.

**Tribal Land:** A concealed handgun license shall not be valid on tribal land, unless authorized by the governing body of an Indian nation, tribe or pueblo. N.M. Stat. Ann. § 29-19-10.

**Open Carry:** New Mexico is an Open Carry State, meaning it is legal to carry a loaded weapon as long as it is not concealed. However, it is not legal to carry any firearm in any federal building, school, state building, or licensed liquor establishment. It is the responsibility of the person carrying the firearm to be informed as to when/where carrying is prohibited. N.M. Stat. Ann. § 30-7-2.

**Alcohol and Drugs:** No person shall carry a concealed handgun while impaired by the use of alcohol, controlled substances, or over-the-counter or prescribed medications. N.M. Admin. Code § 10.8.2

**No Badges:** No person who is not a law enforcement officer, may carry a badge, patch, card, or any other indication of authority to carry a concealed handgun in New Mexico other than the license issued by the department or a license issued by a state that has been accepted by transfer, recognition or reciprocity by New Mexico pursuant to the act. N.M. Admin. Code § 10.8.

**Albuquerque Additional Restrictions**: Under Administrative Instruction No: 5-20 Albuquerque bans firearms in Parks, Recreation Centers and Other Facilities determined to be "school property". Use caution.

# New York

*The New York Constitution contains NO provision for the right to keep and bear arms.*

**Rating:** ★

New York State Police
Troop Headquarters
Building 22, 1220
Washington Avenue
Albany, NY 12226

## Prohibited Areas

### Places Off Limits to Firearms Under State Law:

1. No person, including a handgun license holder, may knowingly possess a firearm in or upon a building or grounds, used for educational purposes, of any school, college or university without the written permission of the institution. (N.Y. Penal Law §265.01(3), §265.20(a)(3))

2. In state parks or forests, except for hunting purposes where permitted (N.Y. Comp. Codes R. & Regs. tit.9, §375.1(p))

3. On the grounds of a residential child care facility (N.Y. Comp. Codes R. & Regs. tit.18, §441.19(f))

4. At any facility of the New York Department of Mental Hygiene, or any residential facility that has an operating certificate issued by the Department (N.Y. Comp. Codes R. & Regs. tit.14, §45.1)

5. At any facility operated or licensed by the Office of Mental Health of the Department of Mental Hygiene (N.Y. Comp. Codes R. & Regs. tit.14, §542.5(a)).

6. Courthouses

7. Cities and municipalities may have additional restrictions.

**Permits Recognized By This State: NONE**

legal

## Special Notes:

**Assault Weapon Ban:** Effective 04-15-14 all grandfathered "assault weapons" must be registered with the State Police. These weapons may no longer be sold in the State of New York effective 04-15-13.

**Magazine Capacity**: Since the federal assault weapons ban in 1994, it has been illegal in New York State to buy, for any gun, a detachable magazine, manufactured after the law took effect that can contain more than ten rounds. Starting April 15, 2013, only magazines that contain 7 rounds or less will be sold in New York, including permanently modified magazines. Starting on April 15, 2013, you are limited to putting only seven rounds in your magazine, unless you are at an incorporated firing range or competition recognized by the National Rifle Association or International Handgun Metallic Silhouette Association, in which case the limit is ten. Large capacity magazines are prohibited. Large capacity ammunition feeding device" means a magazine, belt, drum, feed strip, or similar device, that (A) Has a capacity of, or that can be readily restored or converted to accept, more than ten rounds of ammunition, OR (B) Contains more than seven rounds of ammunition. (N.Y. Penal Law §400.23)

**Preemption of Permits:** All Permits shall be effective throughout the state, except that the same shall not be valid within the city of New York unless a special permit granting validity is issued by the police commissioner of that city. (N.Y. Penal Law §400)

# North Carolina

*"A well regulated militia being necessary to the security of a free State, the right of the people to keep and bear arms shall not be infringed; and, as standing armies in time of peace are dangerous to liberty, they shall not be maintained, and the military shall be kept under strict subordination to, and governed by, the civil power. Nothing herein shall justify the practice of carrying concealed weapons, or prevent the General Assembly from enacting penal statutes against that practice."*

*Art. 1, § 30*

**Rating:** ★ ★ ★

State of North Carolina
Office of the Attorney General
Department of Justice
P.O. Box 629
Raleigh, NC 27602
(919) 716-6400

## Prohibited Areas

### Places Off Limits to Firearms Under State Law:

1. Schools, public or private, all levels including universities. A curricular or extracurricular activity sponsored by a school. This also applies to all property owned by any school. (N.C. Gen Stat. §14-269.2)

2. Assemblies and establishments where admission was charged. (N.C. Gen Stat. §14-269.3)

    a. This law does not apply to permit holders unless the establishment is posted as off limits to firearms.

3. Assemblies and establishments where alcohol is both sold and consumed. (N.C. Gen Stat. §14-269.3)

    a. This law does not apply to permit holders unless the establishment is posted as off limits to firearms.

4. Most state legislative buildings and grounds. State Capitol Building, the Executive Mansion, the Western Residence of the Governor, or on the grounds of any of these buildings, and any building housing any court of the General Court of Justice. (N.C. Gen. Stat. §14-269.4). State office buildings or any portion of a building in which there're State offices. (N.C. Gen. Stat. §14-415.11(c)) **(See special note below for parking lot rules)**.

5. Law Enforcement or Correctional Facilities. (N.C. Gen Stat. §14-415.11(c))

6. Events Occurring in Public: It shall be unlawful for any person participating in, affiliated with, or present as a spectator at any parade, funeral procession, picket line, or demonstration upon any private health care facility or upon any public place owned or under the control of the State or any of its political subdivisions to willfully or intentionally possess or have immediate access to any dangerous weapon. (N.C. Gen Stat. §14-277.2)

7. Courthouses. NC R ORANGE CTY RCRP Rule 17

8. Where notice of carrying a concealed handgun is prohibited by the posting of a conspicuous notice or statement. (N.C. Gen Stat. §14-415.11(c))

9. State owned rest areas/stops, or state hunting/fishing reserves. (N.C. Gen Stat. §14-415.11)

10. Several Game Lands, see the state website for current details.

11. TVA Campgrounds (not including unloaded and encased firearms during hunting season or on a public boat ramp or associated road or parking lot).

12. It shall be lawful for a person to carry any firearm openly, or to carry a concealed handgun with a concealed carry permit, at any State-owned rest area, at any State-owned rest stop along the highways, and at any State-owned hunting and fishing reservation. N.C. Gen. Stat. Ann. § 14-415.11.


**Permits Recognized By This State: ALL STATE PERMITS**


## Special Notes:

**Police Encounters - Duty to Inform:** North Carolina is **a duty to inform state,** which means that you must immediately inform an officer of the presence of a concealed firearm when approached or addressed by and officer, and you must display your permit and identification upon request from the officer.

- **The Law**: The person shall carry the permit together with valid identification whenever the person is carrying a concealed handgun, shall disclose to any law enforcement officer that the person holds a valid permit and is carrying a concealed handgun when approached or addressed by the officer, and shall display both the permit and the proper identification upon the request of a law enforcement officer.
N.C. Gen. Stat. Ann. § 14-415.11

**Must Carry Permit:** A person who has been issued a valid permit who is found to be carrying a concealed handgun without the permit in the person's possession or who fails to disclose to any law enforcement officer that the person holds a valid permit and is carrying a concealed handgun, as required by G.S. 14-415.11, shall be guilty of an infraction and shall be punished in accordance with G.S. 14-3.1. N.C. Gen. Stat. Ann. § 14-415.21

**Parking lot rule for state legislative grounds:** *No rule adopted under this section shall prohibit the transportation or storage of a firearm in a closed compartment or container within a person's locked vehicle or in a locked container securely affixed to a person's vehicle. Notwithstanding any other provision of law, a legislator or legislative employee who parks a vehicle in a State-owned parking space that is leased or assigned to that legislator or legislative employee may transport a firearm to the parking space and store that firearm in the vehicle parked in the parking space, provided that: (i) the firearm is in a closed compartment or container within the legislator's or legislative employee's locked vehicle, or (ii) the firearm is in a locked container securely affixed to the legislator or legislative employee's vehicle.* (N.C. Gen. Stat. Ann. §120-32.1 (West))

**Alcohol:** It shall be unlawful for any person, with or without a permit, to carry a concealed handgun while consuming alcohol or at any time while the person has remaining in his or her blood a controlled substance previously consumed, unless the controlled substance in the person's blood was lawfully obtained and taken in therapeutically appropriate amounts or if the person is on the person's own property. (N.C. Gen Stat. §14-415.11(c)(2))

# North Dakota

*"All individuals are by nature equally free and independent and have certain inalienable rights, among which are those of enjoying and defending life and liberty; acquiring, possessing and protecting property and reputation; pursuing and obtaining safety and happiness; and to keep and bear arms for the defense of their person, family, property, and the state, and for lawful hunting, recreational, and other lawful purposes, which shall not be infringed"*

*Art. I, § 1*

**Rating:** ★ ★ ★

North Dakota
Office of the Attorney General
Bureau of Criminal Investigation
P.O. Box 1054
Bismark, ND 58503
(701) 328-5500

## Prohibited Areas

### Places Off Limits to Firearms Under State Law:

1. That part of an establishment that is set aside for the retail sale of alcoholic beverages or used as a gaming site at which bingo is the primary gaming activity. This prohibition does not apply to the restaurant part of an establishment if individuals under the age of 21 are also allowed in that portion of the restaurant. (N.D. Cent. Code §62.1-02-04)

2. Gaming sites (N.D. Cent. Code §62.1-02-05(1))

3. State game refuge or state game management area (N.D. Cent. Code §20.1-11-13(3))

4. Sporting events (N.D. Cent. Code §62.1-02-05(1))

5. Public and private schools (N.D. Cent. Code §62.1-02-05(1))

6. Churches or church functions (N.D. Cent. Code §62.1-02-05(1))

   a. The above prohibition relating to churches does not apply to: "An individual possessing a valid class 1 concealed weapons license from this state or who has reciprocity (through an out-of-state permit) authorizing the individual to carry a dangerous weapon concealed if the individual is in a church building or other place of worship and has the approval to carry in the church building or other place of worship by a primary religious leader of the church or other place of worship or the governing body of the church or other place of worship. If a church or other place of worship authorizes an individual to carry a concealed weapon, local law enforcement must be informed of the name of the authorized individual" (N.D. Cent. Code §62.1-02-05(2)(j))

7. Political rallies and events (N.D. Cent. Code §62.1-02-05(1))

8. Concerts (N.D. Cent. Code §62.1-02-05(1))

9. While on the Capitol grounds or in any building on the Capitol grounds without written approval. ND OMB Policy Number 02-89

10. Public gatherings (N.D. Cent. Code §62.1-02-05(1))

    a. "public gathering" includes athletic or sporting events, schools or school functions, churches or church functions, political rallies or functions, musical concerts, and individuals in publicly owned parks where hunting is not allowed by proclamation and publicly owned or operated buildings. The term "public gathering" does not apply to a state or federal park.

**Permits Recognized By This State:** Alabama, Alaska, Arizona, Arkansas, Colorado, Delaware, Florida, Georgia, Idaho, Indiana, Iowa, Kansas, Kentucky, Louisiana, Maine, Michigan, Mississippi, Missouri, Montana, Nebraska, Nevada, New Hampshire, New Mexico, North Carolina, Ohio, Oklahoma, Pennsylvania, South Carolina, South Dakota, Tennessee, Texas, Utah, Washington, West Virginia, Wisconsin, Wyoming

## Special Notes:

**Police Encounters - Quasi Duty to Inform:** North Dakota is a quasi duty to inform state if you have a permit (although it is a duty to inform state if you do not have a permit), which means that you are not affirmatively required to tell a police officer that you have a firearm in your possession, but if you are asked by an officer during a lawful stop you must provide them with your permit.

- **The Law**: Every individual while carrying a concealed firearm or dangerous weapon, for which a license to carry concealed is required, shall have on one's person the license issued by this or another state and shall give it to any active law enforcement officer for an inspection upon demand by the officer. The failure of any individual to give the license to the officer is prima facie evidence the individual is illegally carrying a firearm or dangerous weapon concealed. N.D. Cent. Code Ann. § 62.1-04-04

**Constitutional Carry:** Effective 08/01/17 North Dakota **residents** may carry a loaded concealed firearm without a permit. The following are the eligibility requirements for an individual to carry concealed in North Dakota without a concealed weapon license:

- Must be at least 18 years of age.
- Must be a resident of North Dakota for 1 year as evidenced by ND drivers license or ND ID card.
- Not prohibited by state or federal law from possessing a firearm.
- ND drivers license or ND ID card must be carried (or the individual must have a digital image of the license).
- If carrying under this provision, **the individual MUST inform law enforcement that they are in possession of the firearm upon any in-person contact by a law enforcement officer**.
- Restrictions on location (places) that a firearm may be possessed or carried by law (N.D.C.C. Title 62.1) still apply.

**Vehicle Storage:** Employees may store their firearms in locked personal vehicles on publicly accessible parking lots without fear of being fired.  This law also protects customers who have firearms locked in their private vehicles.  (N.D. Cent. Code §62.102– 2011 HB 1438)

**Permitless Vehicle Carry:** On December 14, 2017 the North Dakota Attorney General issued the following opinion: "It is my opinion, that an individual's valid driver's license or sanctioned identification card is the equivalent of a "valid concealed weapons license" as required under N.D.C.C. § 62.1 - 02 - 10 with regard to what was previously only known as a class 2 concealed weapons license." 2017-L-07

# Ohio

*"The people have the right to bear arms for their defense and security; but standing armies, in time of peace, are dangerous to liberty, and shall not be kept up; and the military shall be in strict subordination to the civil power."*

*Art. I, § 4*

**Rating:** ★ ★ ★

State of Ohio
Office of the Attorney General
30 E. Broad Street
Columbus, OH 43215
(614) 466-4320

## Prohibited Areas

**Places Off Limits to Firearms Under State Law:**

1.  Police stations. (Ohio Rev. Code. Ann. §2923.126(b))

2.  Sheriffs' offices. (Ohio Rev. Code. Ann. §2923.126(b))

3.  Highway Patrol posts. (Ohio Rev. Code. Ann. §2923.126(b))

4.  Premises controlled by the Ohio Bureau of Criminal Identification and Investigation. (Ohio Rev. Code. Ann. §2923.126(b))

5.  Correctional institutions or other detention facilities. (Ohio Rev. Code. Ann. §2923.126(b))

6.  Airport terminals or commercial airplanes. (Ohio Rev. Code. Ann. §2923.126(b))

    a.  Effective 03/18/17 this prohibition only pertains to any area of an airport passenger terminal that is beyond a passenger or property screening checkpoint or to which access is restricted through security measures by the airport authority or a public agency

7.  Institutions for the care of mentally ill persons. (Ohio Rev. Code. Ann. §2923.126(b))

8.  Courthouses or buildings in which a courtroom is located. (Ohio Rev. Code. Ann. §2923.126(b))

9.  Universities, unless locked in a motor vehicle or in the process of being locked in a motor vehicle. (Ohio Rev. Code. Ann. §2923.126(b))

10. Places of worship, unless the place of worship permits otherwise. (Ohio Rev. Code. Ann. §2923.126(b))

11. Licensed D-Liquor Permit premises.

    a.  a concealed carry license holder may possess a firearm in a liquor permit premises, or an open air arena, for which a D permit has been issued if the permit holder is not consuming beer or intoxicating liquor or under the influence of alcohol or a drug of abuse.

12. Government facilities that are not used primarily as a shelter, restroom, parking facility for motor vehicles, or rest facility and is not a courthouse or a

building or structure in which a courtroom is located. (Ohio Rev. Code. Ann. §2923.126(b))

    a. Unless the governing body with authority over the building has enacted a statute, ordinance, or policy that permits a licensee to carry

13. School safety zones. (Ohio Rev. Code. Ann. §2923.126(b))

    a. Effective 03/18/17 this section does not apply to a person if all of the following apply: (a) The person is carrying a valid concealed handgun license or the person is an active duty member of the armed forces of the United States and is carrying a valid military identification card and documentation of successful completion of firearms training that meets or exceeds the training. (b) The person leaves the handgun in a motor vehicle. (c) The handgun does not leave the motor vehicle. (d) If the person exits the motor vehicle, the person locks the motor vehicle.

14. Capitol buildings and grounds. (Ohio Admin Code 128-4-02)

15. Posted buildings. (Ohio Rev. Code. Ann. §2923.126(C)(3)(a))

**Permits Recognized By This State: ALL STATE PERMITS**

**Special Notes:**

**Police Encounters - Duty to Inform: Ohio has a duty to inform law relating to traffic stops and a quasi duty to inform law for all other law enforcement encounters**. This means if you are pulled over while operating a vehicle you must affirmatively and immediately inform an officer that you have a permit and you have a weapon in the vehicle. In all other instances where you encounter an officer you must only provide your permit and identification if requested by an officer.

- **The Law While Driving - Duty To Inform**: It is a crime to fail to promptly inform any law enforcement officer who approaches the vehicle while stopped that the person has been issued a concealed handgun license and that the person then possesses or has a loaded handgun in the motor vehicle; Ohio Rev. Code Ann. § 2923.16

- **The Law Other Than Driving - Quasi Duty To Inform**: The licensee must carry the license, together with valid identification, at all times in which the licensee is in actual possession of a concealed weapon or firearm and must display both the license and proper identification upon demand by a law enforcement officer. Fla. Stat. Ann. § 790.06

**Landlords:** A landlord may not prohibit or restrict a tenant who is a licensee from lawfully carrying or possessing a handgun on those residential premises. Ohio Rev. Code Ann. § 2923.126 (b)

# Oklahoma

*"The right of a citizen to keep and bear arms in defense of his home, person, or property, or in aid of the civil power, when thereunto legally summoned, shall never be prohibited; but nothing herein contained shall prevent the Legislature from regulating the carrying of weapons. "*

Art. II, § 26

**Rating:** ★ ★ ★

Oklahoma Bureau of Investigation
6600 North Harvey
Oklahoma City, OK 73116
(405) 848-6724

## Prohibited Areas

### Places Off Limits to Firearms Under State Law:

It shall be unlawful for any person in possession of a valid handgun license to carry any concealed or unconcealed handgun into any of the following places:

1. Any structure, building, or office space which is owned or leased by a city, town, county, state or federal governmental authority for the purpose of conducting business with the public;

2. Any courthouse, courtroom, prison, jail, detention facility or any facility used to process, hold or house arrested persons, prisoners or persons alleged delinquent or adjudicated delinquent;

3. Any public or private elementary or public or private secondary school, except as provided below

   a. A concealed or unconcealed weapon may be carried onto private school property or in any school bus or motor vehicle used by any private school for transportation of students or teachers by a person who is licensed pursuant to the Oklahoma Self-Defense Act, provided a policy has been adopted by the governing entity of the private school that authorizes the carrying and possession of a weapon on private school property or in any school bus or motor vehicle used by a private school.

4. Any publicly owned or operated sports arena or venue during a professional sporting event, unless allowed by the event holder;

5. Any place where gambling is authorized by law, unless allowed by the property owner; Okla. Stat. Ann. tit. 21, § 1277

6. Any college, university or technology center school property, unless in accordance with established guidelines

7. Any establishment where low-point beer or alcoholic beverages are consumed.

   a. A person possessing a valid concealed handgun license may carry a concealed handgun into any restaurant or other establishment licensed to dispense low-point beer or alcoholic beverages where the sale of low-point beer or alcoholic beverages does not constitute the primary purpose of the business. Okla. Stat. Ann. tit. 21, § 1272.1

**Permits Recognized By This State: ALL STATE PERMITS**

## Special Notes:

**Police Encounters - Duty to Inform:** Oklahoma is **a duty to inform state,** which means that you must immediately inform an officer of the presence of a concealed firearm when approached or addressed by and officer.

- **The Law**: It shall be unlawful for any person to fail or refuse to identify the fact that the person is in actual possession of a concealed or unconcealed handgun when the person comes into contact with any law enforcement officer of this state or its political subdivisions or a federal law enforcement officer during the course of any arrest, detainment, or routine traffic stop. Said identification to the law enforcement officer shall be made at the first opportunity. No person shall be required to identify himself or herself as a handgun licensee when no handgun is in the possession of the person or in any vehicle in which the person is driving or is a passenger.

**Constitutional (Permitless) Carry**: Effective November 1, 2019 Oklahoma became a *constitutional carry* state. Anyone over the age of 21 (or 18 if in the military) who is otherwise not prohibited from possessing a firearm may do so without a permit.

- **The Law:** The law shall not prohibit...The carrying of a firearm, concealed or unconcealed, loaded or unloaded, by a person who is twenty-one (21) years of age or older or by a person who is eighteen (18) years of age but not yet twenty-one (21) years of age and the person is a member or veteran of the United States Armed Forces, Reserves or National Guard or was discharged under honorable conditions from the United States Armed Forces, Reserves or National Guard, and the person is otherwise not disqualified from the possession or purchase of a firearm under state or federal law and is not carrying the firearm in furtherance of a crime. Okla. Stat. Ann. tit. 21, § 1272 (6)

**Places NOT Off Limits:** The law regarding prohibited places does not include, and specifically excludes, the following property:

- Any property set aside for the use or parking of any motor vehicle, whether attended or unattended, by a city, town, county, state or federal governmental authority;

- Any property set aside for the use or parking of any motor vehicle, whether attended or unattended, which is open to the public or by any entity engaged in gambling authorized by law;

- Any property adjacent to a structure, building or office space in which concealed or unconcealed weapons are prohibited by the provisions of this section;

- Any property designated by a city, town, county or state governmental authority as a park, recreational area, or fairgrounds; provided, nothing in this paragraph shall be construed to authorize any entry by a person in possession of a concealed or unconcealed handgun into any structure, building or office space which is specifically prohibited by the provisions of subsection A of this section; and

- Any property set aside by a public or private elementary or secondary school for the use or parking of any motor vehicle, whether attended or unattended; provided, however, said handgun shall be stored and hidden from view in a locked motor vehicle when the motor vehicle is left unattended on school property.

**Must Possess Permit & Photo ID:** The person shall be required to have possession of his or her valid handgun license or valid military identification card as provided for qualified persons in this section and a valid Oklahoma driver license or an Oklahoma State photo identification at all times when in possession of an authorized pistol. The person shall display the handgun license or a valid military identification card on demand of a law enforcement officer; provided, however, that in the absence of reasonable and articulable suspicion of other criminal activity, an individual carrying an unconcealed or concealed handgun shall not be disarmed or physically restrained unless the individual fails to display a valid handgun license or a valid military identification card as provided for qualified persons in this section in response to that demand.
Okla. Stat. Ann. tit. 21, § 1290.8

**Vehicle Storage:** No person, property owner, tenant, employer, or business entity shall be permitted to establish any policy or rule that has the effect of prohibiting any person, except a convicted felon, from transporting and storing firearms in a locked vehicle on any property set aside for any vehicle. (Okla. Stat. tit.21, §1290.22)

- Oklahoma "Parking Lot" firearm storage protections applies to vehicles parked at professional sporting events, local, state governmental entities, and on vocational-technology center campuses. (2011 HB 1652 – amends Okla. Stat. tit.21, §1277). Parking lot storage is allowed in these places.

**Alcohol & Prescription Drugs:** It shall be unlawful for any person to carry or use shotguns, rifles or pistols in any circumstances while under the influence of beer, intoxicating liquors or any hallucinogenic, or any unlawful or un prescribed drug, and it shall be unlawful for any person to carry or use shotguns, rifles or pistols when under the influence of any drug prescribed by a licensed physician if the aftereffects of such consumption affect mental, emotional or physical processes to a degree that would result in abnormal behavior. (Okla. Stat. tit.21, §1289.9)

# Oregon

*"The people shall have the right to bear arms for the defense of themselves, and the State, but the Military shall be kept in strict subordination to the civil power."*

*Art. I, § 27*

**Rating:** ★ ★ ★

## Prohibited Areas

### Places Off Limits to Firearms Under State Law:

1. Court Facilities (Or. Rev. Stat. §166.370)
   a. "Court facility" means a courthouse or that portion of any other building occupied by a circuit court, the Court of Appeals, the Supreme Court or the Oregon Tax Court or occupied by personnel related to the operations of those courts, or in which activities related to the operations of those courts take place. Or. Rev. Stat. § 166.360
2. Correctional facilities (Or. Admin. R. 291-016-0030(5))
3. Certified childcare centers. (Or. Admin. R. 414-300-0170(1)(k))
4. Racecourses (Or. Admin. R. 462-130-0010(1)(w))
5. Schools (Or. Rev. Stat. §166.370, see special note below for exceptions)
6. Property of Oregon Commission for the Blind, including vehicles (Or. Admin. R. 585-001-0010(1)(c))
7. On property owned or controlled by the Oregon State Fair and Exposition Center (Or. Admin. R. 736-201-0060(1)(d)); (Potentially does not apply to permit holders, see Or. Admin. R. 736-201-0060(2)(a))

### Permits Recognized By This State: NONE

## Special Notes:

**Non-Resident Permits:** Although Oregon does not recognize any other state's concealed firearm permits, certain counties may issue a nonresident permit to residents of bordering states. Namely Washington, California, Nevada and Idaho.

**Public Buildings:** Or. Rev. Stat. §166.370(3)(d) allows a person who is licensed under Or. Rev. Stat. §166.291 and §166.292 to carry in public buildings (hospitals, capitol buildings, state office buildings, etc). **HOWEVER**, Or. Rev. Stat. §166.380 states that, *"A peace officer may examine a firearm possessed by anyone on the person while in or on a public building to determine whether the firearm is a loaded firearm. Refusal by a person to allow the examination authorized by subsection (1) of this section constitutes reason to believe that the person has committed a crime and the peace officer may make an arrest pursuant to Or. Rev. Stat. §133.310."* No exemption is given for permit holders to this requirement and its exact applicability to permit holders is unknown. As it appears to our reading, a permit holder, while in a public building, may be required to maintain the firearm "unloaded" or at least submit to an inspection of the firearm when asked by a peace officer therein. (see Or. Rev. Stat. § 166.380). We encourage individual due diligence in determining how the firearm must be carried into a public building.

**Schools:** Or. Rev. Stat. Ann. § 166.360 defines a "Public building" as a hospital, a capitol building, a public or private school, a college or university, a city hall or the residence of any state official elected by the state at large, and the grounds adjacent to each such building. The term also includes that portion of any other building occupied by an agency of the state or a municipal corporation, other than a court facility. Or. Rev. Stat. Ann. § 166.370(3)(g) exempts "A person who is licensed to carry a concealed handgun" from the prohibition against carrying a firearm in public buildings. Additionally, firearms may be possessed on school property if they are: A) possessed by a person who is not otherwise prohibited from possessing the firearm; and (B) the firearm is unloaded and locked in a motor vehicle.

- **Firearms on Public College Campuses:** The Oregon Court of Appeals ruled in late 2011 that the OUS' administrative rule, OAR 580-022-0045(3), which prohibits firearms and other weapons from campuses, is invalid. Specifically, the Court ruled, "we conclude that OAR 580−022−0045(3) is an exercise of an "authority to regulate" firearms that is not expressly authorized by the Legislative Assembly, and that it is preempted by ORS 166.170(1). Accordingly, the rule exceeds the agency's authority, ORS 183.400(4)(b), and is invalid." Oregon Firearms Educ. Found. v. Bd. of Higher Educ., 245 Or. App. 713, 723, 264 P.3d 160, 165 (2011). However, despite the court ruling the Oregon State Board of Education continues to ban firearms on college campuses, claiming authority under 2012's Senate Bill 242.

**Cities and Counties**: A city or county may adopt ordinances to regulate, restrict or prohibit the possession of loaded firearms in public buildings as defined in Or. Rev. Stat. §161.015. (§166.173(1)). However, due to the exemption of permit holders under Or. Rev. Stat. §166.370(3) the Oregon Attorney General has stated that "*the legislature did not intend...to allow local governments to negate the right granted by the statute to concealed handgun licensees."* 46 Or. Op. Atty. Gen. 362, 1990 WL 519208 (Or. A.G. 1990) **and thus these prohibitions do not apply to permit holders**.

**Knives and other non-firearm weapons:** Except for peace officers, any person who carries concealed upon the person any knife having a blade that projects or swings into position by force of a spring or by centrifugal force, any dirk, dagger, ice pick, slingshot, metal knuckles, or any similar instrument by the use of which injury could be inflicted upon the person or property of any other person, commits a Class B misdemeanor. (Or. Rev. Stat. §166.240). "Like a gun in a holster, a knife carried openly in a sheath on the belt is not "concealed." State v. Johnson, 772 P.2d 426, 428 (Or. App. 1989).

# Pennsylvania

*"The right of the citizens to bear arms in defense of themselves and the State shall not be questioned."*

Art. 1, § 21

**Rating:** ★ ★ ★ ★

Commonwealth of Pennsylvania
Office of the Attorney General
Strawberry Square
Harrisburg, PA 17120
(717) 787-3391

## Prohibited Areas

### Places Off Limits to Firearms Under State Law:

1. Courthouses (18 Pa. Cons. Stat. §913)

2. Public and private school property (18 Pa. Cons. Stat. §913)

3. Detention centers (police, sheriff, and prison) (61 Pa. Cons. Stat. §5902)

4. Mental hospital (18 Pa. Consol. Stat. Ann. § 5122)

5. The Capitol Complex (49 Pa. Cons. Stat. §61.1)

   a. The possession of firearms or other prohibited offensive weapons as defined in 18 Pa.C.S. § 908(c) (relating to prohibited offense weapons), while on the leased premises of the Department with the exception of State or Federal officers, in connection with the performance of an official duty, is prohibited. This prohibition does not apply to attorneys listed as counsel of record in connection with the offering of an exhibit in any administrative proceeding, if the counsel of record who intends to offer the item as an exhibit, has obtained written authorization from a hearing examiner to do so. 49 Pa. Code § 61.3

**Permits Recognized By This State:** Alabama, Alaska, Arizona, Arkansas, Colorado, Florida, Georgia, Idaho (enhanced permit only), Indiana, Iowa, Kansas, Kentucky, Louisiana, Michigan, Mississippi, Missouri, Montana, New Hampshire, North Carolina, North Dakota (Class I only), Ohio, Oklahoma, South Dakota, Tennessee, Texas, Utah, West Virginia, Wisconsin, Wyoming.

**Permits issued to *non-residents* of the above listed states, or to individuals *under the age of 21*, are *not* recognized by Pennsylvania**

## Special Notes:

**Vehicles**: Pennsylvania law provides that "any person who carries a firearm in any vehicle...without a valid and lawfully issued license...commits a felony." 18 Pa.Cons. Stat. Ann. § 6106(a).

**Age to Carry:** Subject to certain exceptions, a person under the age of 18 shall not possess or transport a firearm anywhere in the Commonwealth. 18 Pa. Cons. Stat. Ann. §6110.1(a).

**Hunting.** It is lawful for any person who possesses a valid license to carry a firearm issued under 18 Cons. Stat. §6109 to carry that firearm while hunting (including bow hunting) in Pennsylvania. T. 34 §2525

**Other Weapons**: A PA license to carry firearms does not include dirks, knives, or batons.

**Pennsylvania Permit Required for Pennsylvania Residents:** A PA resident who wants to carry a concealed weapon must have a PA permit. Obtaining a permit from a reciprocal state does not allow a PA resident to concealed carry. Again, a PA resident must have a PA permit. ( V. McKown, 2013 PA Super 282, 2013 WL 5729802).

**State Parks:** You must have a valid license to conceal or open carry in Pennsylvania state parks. (18 Pa. Cons. Stat. Ann. §6109(m.2), (m.3) & (n)).

# Rhode Island

*"The right of the people to keep and bear arms shall not be infringed."*

*Art. 1, § 22*

**Rating:** ★

State of Rhode Island
Office of the Attorney General
Bureau of Criminal Investigation
150 South Main Street
Providence, RI 02903
(401) 274-4400

## Prohibited Areas

**Places Off Limits to Firearms Under State Law:**

1. School grounds (R.I. Gen Laws §11-47-60(a))

2. State parks (R.I. Gen Laws §12-080-052)

3. State child care program facilities (R.I. Gen Laws §03-000-014)

4. Possession of a firearm or archery equipment is prohibited on Public Reservations, unless the person is duly licensed to hunt, is engaged in authorized hunting activity and is in possession of a firearm or archery equipment authorized pursuant to the governing RIDEM hunting regulations for the specific hunting activity in which the person is engaged. 250-RICR-100-00-1 (1.17)

   a. Possession of a loaded firearm, archery equipment having a nocked arrow or bolt, or firearm with magazine or chamber from which all shells or cartridges have not been removed, located in or on any vehicle or conveyance while in or upon any part of a Public Reservation is prohibited unless possessed by a law enforcement officer

**Note**: Rhode Island law states persons licensed to carry a concealed firearm shall "have the right to carry concealed firearms everywhere within this state; provided, that this shall not be construed as giving the right to carry concealed firearms to a person transporting firearms as merchandise or as household or business goods." (R.I. Gen Laws §11-47-9). However, permit holders are advised to comply with the above prohibitions.

**Permits Recognized By This State: NONE**

## Special Notes:

**Carrying While Intoxicated:** It is unlawful to carry or transport any firearm in this state when intoxicated or under the influence of intoxicating liquor or narcotic drugs. R.I. Gen. Laws Ann. § 11-47-52

# South Carolina

*"A well regulated militia being necessary to the security of a free State, the right of the people to keep and bear arms shall not be infringed. As, in times of peace, armies are dangerous to liberty, they shall not be maintained without the consent of the General Assembly. The military power of the State shall always be held in subordination to the civil authority and be governed by it."*

*Art. 1, § 20*

**Rating:** ★ ★ ★

State of South Carolina
State Law Enforcement
Division P.O. Box 21398
Columbia, SC 29221
(803) 737-9000

## Prohibited Areas

### Places Off Limits to Firearms Under State Law:

1. Police, sheriff, or highway patrol station or any other law enforcement office or facility (S.C. Code Ann. §23-31-215(M))

2. Detention facility, prison, or jail or any other correctional facility or office (S.C. Code Ann. §23-31-215(M))

3. Restaurants that serve alcohol **IF drinking** (SC Code Ann. §16-23-465)

4. Courthouse or courtroom (S.C. Code Ann. §23-31-215(M))

5. Polling place on election days (S.C. Code Ann. §23-31-215(M))

6. Office of or the business meeting of the governing body of a county, public school district, municipality, or special purpose district (S.C. Code Ann. §23-31-215(M))

7. School or college athletic event not related to firearms (S.C. Code Ann. §23-31-215(M))

8. Daycare facility or preschool facility (S.C. Code Ann. §23-31-215(M))

9. Church or other established religious sanctuary unless express permission is given by the appropriate church official or governing body (S.C. Code Ann. §23-31-215(M))

10. Bus or other public transit (S.C. Code Ann. §11-47-60(a))

11. State capitol (SC Code Ann. § 10-11-320)

12. The residence or dwelling place of another without permission (SC Code Ann. §23-31-225)

13. Hospital, medical clinic, doctor's office, or any other facility where medical services or procedures are performed unless expressly authorized by the employer. (S.C. Code Ann. §23-31-215(M))

14. Elementary and secondary school property (S.C. Code Ann. §23-31-215(M))

15. Premises or property owned, operated, or controlled by a private or public school, college, university, technical college, other post-secondary institution, or in any publicly-owned building, without the express permission of the authorities in charge of the premises or property. Permit holders may have firearm in attended or locked vehicle while secured in case (if in trunk) or locked compartment. (S.C. Code Ann. §16-23-420)

16. "Posted" buildings in accordance with S.C. Code Ann. §23-31-235 (see special note below)

**Permits Recognized By This State:** Alaska, Arizona, Arkansas, Florida, Georgia, Idaho (Enhanced permit carried by Idaho residents only), Kansas, Kentucky, Louisiana, Michigan, Mississippi (enhanced permit only), Missouri, New Mexico, North Carolina, North Dakota, Ohio, Oklahoma, South Dakota (Enhanced Permit Only), Texas, Tennessee, West Virginia, Wyoming.

**Note: South Carolina Only Recognizes Permits Issued To Residents Of The Above States, No Non-Resident Permits.**

## Special Notes:

**Police Encounters - Duty to Inform:** South Carolina is **a duty to inform state,** which means that you must immediately inform an officer of the presence of a concealed firearm when contacted in an official capacity and the officer requests your identification.

- **The Law**: A permit holder must have his permit identification card in his possession whenever he carries a concealable weapon. When carrying a concealable weapon a permit holder must inform a law enforcement officer of the fact that he is a permit holder and present the permit identification card when an officer: (1) identifies himself as a law enforcement officer; and (2) requests identification or a driver's license from a permit holder. S.C. Code Ann. § 23-31-215

**Vehicle Transport:** In South Carolina a non-permittee may transport a firearm in his vehicle in the following manner:

- **S.C. Code Ann. §16-23-20(9)** a person in a vehicle if the handgun is secured in a closed glove compartment, closed console, closed trunk, or in a closed container secured by an integral fastener and transported in the luggage compartment of the vehicle; however, this item is not violated if the glove compartment, console, or trunk is opened in the presence of a law enforcement officer for the sole purpose of retrieving a driver's license, registration, or proof of insurance;

**Posted Building Law**: A Posted building must have a sign that meets the following requirements: All signs must be posted at each entrance into a building where a concealable weapon permit holder is prohibited from carrying a concealable weapon and must be: **(1)** clearly visible from outside the building; **(2)** eight inches wide by twelve inches tall in size; **(3)** contain the words "NO CONCEALABLE WEAPONS ALLOWED" in black one-inch tall uppercase type at the bottom of the sign and centered between the lateral edges of the sign; **(4)** contain a black silhouette of a handgun inside a circle seven inches in diameter with a diagonal line that runs from the lower left to the upper right at a forty-five degree angle from the horizontal; **(5)** a diameter of a circle (S.C. Code Ann. §23-31-235)

**Carrying in a Residence or Dwelling:** A person licensed to carry a concealed handgun must have the express permission of the homeowner – or person in legal control – in order to carry the firearm in the residence. (S.C. Code Ann. §23-31-225).

**Preemption**: There have been some municipalities in South Carolina that have attempted to implement restrictive firearms laws beyond what state law mandates. On September 17, 2019, for example, the city of Columbia adopted ordinance 2019-063 which prohibits the possession of firearms within 1,000 feet of a school. On December 2, 2019 Attorney General Alan Wilson issued an opinion that the city ordinance, at least in large part, is invalid under S.C. Code Ann. § 23-31-510 and 520.

## South Dakota

*"The right of the citizens to bear arms in defense of themselves and the state shall not be denied"*

*Art. VI, § 24*

**Rating:** ★ ★ ★ ★

State of South Dakota
Office of Secretary of State
500 East Capitol Avenue
Pierre, SD 57501

## Prohibited Areas

### Places Off Limits to Firearms Under State Law:

1. County courthouse (S.D. Codified Laws §22-14-23). An exception to this prohibition exists for someone with an enhanced permit who notifies the superintendent of the Division of Highway Patrol 24 hours in advance. See §22-14-24 for more details.

2. Elementary or secondary school premises, including school vehicles or buildings (S.D. Codified Laws §13-32-7)

3. Game preserve or refuge, unless the permit holder is:

    a. On a public highway and the firearm is enclosed in a case; or

    b. A resident within the preserve or refuge and is carrying the firearm to use against non-game and predatory animals or birds on his or her own premises. (S.D. Codified Laws §41-5-8)

4. A person may not carry a concealed pistol in any licensed on-sale malt beverage or alcoholic beverage establishment that derives over one-half of its total income from the sale of malt or alcoholic beverages. S.D. Codified Laws § 23-7-70

**Permits Recognized By This State: ALL STATE PERMITS**

## Special Notes:

**Permitless ("Constitutional") Carry:** Effective 07/01/19 South Dakota became a true permitless ("Constitutional") carry state. What this means is that anyone who can otherwise legally possess a firearm may carry it concealed in South Dakota without a permit.

- **The Law:** The issuance of a permit to carry a concealed pistol under this chapter, or the recognition of nonresident permits to carry a concealed pistol does not impose a general prohibition on the carry of a pistol without a permit. S.D. Codified Laws § 23-7-7.

- Any valid permit to carry a concealed pistol, issued to a nonresident of South Dakota, is valid in South Dakota according to the terms of its issuance in the state of its issue, but only to the extent that the terms of issuance comply with any appropriate South Dakota statute or promulgated rule. This section does not require a nonresident of this state who may lawfully possess a pistol to have a permit in order to carry a concealed pistol in this state. S.D. Codified Laws § 23-7-7.4

**ATVs**:

- **Motorcycles or Off-Road Vehicles**: No person, other than a law enforcement officer or conservation officer, or any person on the person's own land or land leased by the person, may operate or ride on any motorcycle or off-road vehicle with any firearm in the person's possession unless the firearm is completely unloaded and within a carrying case which encloses the entire firearm. However, this section does not apply to any person who is carrying a pistol and possesses a permit to carry a concealed pistol. S.D. Codified Laws § 32-20-6.6

**School Property**: Any person, other than a law enforcement officer or school sentinel who intentionally carries, possesses, stores, keeps, leaves, places, or puts into the possession of another person, any dangerous weapon, firearm, or air gun, whether or not the firearm or air gun is designed, adapted, used, or intended to be used primarily for imitative or noisemaking purposes, on or in any public elementary or secondary school premises, vehicle, or building, or on or in any premises, vehicle, or building used or leased for public elementary or secondary school functions, whether or not any person is endangered by any action under this section, is guilty of a Class 1 misdemeanor. The provisions of this section do not apply to;

(1) Use of a starting gun at an athletic event;
(2) Any firearm or air gun at a:
(a) Firing range;
(b) Gun show;
(c) Supervised school or session for training in the use of firearms; or
(d) Ceremonial presence of unloaded weapons at color guard ceremonies;
(3) Any nonpublic school;
(4) Any church or other house of worship; or
(5) Any nonpublic school located on the premises of a church or other house of worship.

S.D. Codified Laws § 13-32-7

# Tennessee

*"That the citizens of this State have a right to keep and to bear arms for their common defense; but the Legislature shall have power, by law, to regulate the wearing of arms with a view to prevent crime."*

*Art. I, § 26*

**Rating:** ★ ★ ★ ★

State of Tennessee
Department of Safety
Handgun Division
1150 Foster Avenue
Nashville, TN 37249
(615) 251-8590

## Prohibited Areas

### Places Off Limits to Firearms Under State Law:

1. Any room in which judicial proceedings are in progress.

2. Any public or private school building or bus, on any public or private school campus, grounds, recreation area, athletic field or any other property owned, used or operated by any board of education, school, college or university board of trustees, regents or directors for the administration of any public or private educational institution.

   a. This prohibition also includes carrying onto portions of a religious institution being used for school property, while being used for school purposes. AG Opinion No. 15-67

3. Prisons or correctional facilities (Tenn. Code Ann. §39-16-201)

4. Posted Buildings (Tenn. Code Ann. §39-17-1359)

   a. An individual, corporation, business entity or local, state or federal government entity or agent thereof is authorized to prohibit the possession of weapons by any person. They must display a sign in prominent locations, including all entrances primarily used by persons entering the building, portion of the building or buildings where weapon possession is prohibited. (Tenn. Code Ann. §39-17-1359)

5. A permittee MAY carry into a restaurant that sells alcohol, however a permittee MAY NOT drink while in possession of a firearm. (Tenn. Code Ann. §57-3-204(c)(3))

6. School-administered child-care programs. (Tenn. Comp. R. & Regs. R. 0520-12-1-.14(5)(a)(3)(xii); R. 0520-12-1-.10(4)(f))

7. Group child-care homes (Tenn. Comp. R. & Regs. R. 1240-4-1-.06(4)(k))

8. Drop-In child care centers (Tenn. Comp. R. & Regs. R. 1240-4-2-.08(8)(c))

9. Child care centers (Tenn. Comp. R. & Regs. R. 1240-4-3-.10(13)(d))

10. Family child care homes (Tenn. Comp. R. & Regs. R. 1240-4-4-.06(4)(k))

11. Residential child caring agencies (Tenn. Comp. R. & Regs. R. 1240-4-5-.04(3)(b)(1)(iii)(VII))

**Permits Recognized By This State: ALL STATE PERMITS**

## Special Notes:

### Permitless Vehicle Carry:

- Anyone of legal age may possess a loaded handgun in a vehicle so long as (1) the person is not otherwise prohibited; and (2) the motor vehicle is privately-owned. Tenn. Code Ann. § 39-17-1307(e).

### Weapons Allowed To Be Carried:

- A facially valid handgun permit, firearms permit, weapons permit or license issued by another state shall be valid in this state according to its terms and shall be treated as if it is a handgun permit issued by this state; provided, however, this subsection (r) shall not be construed to authorize the holder of any out-of-state permit or license to carry, in this state, any firearm or weapon other than a handgun. Tenn. Code Ann. § 39-17-1351

# Texas

*"Every citizen shall have the right to keep and bear arms in the lawful defense of himself or the State; but the Legislature shall have power, by law, to regulate the wearing of arms, with a view to prevent crime."*

*Art. I, § 23*

**Rating:** ★ ★ ★ ★

Texas Department of
Public Safety
Concealed Handgun
Licensing Section
Box 4087
Austin, TX 78773
(615) 251-8590

## Prohibited Areas

### Places Off Limits to Firearms Under State Law:

1. A place of business that derives 51% or more of its income from the sale or service of alcoholic beverages for on premises consumption (Tex. Penal Code Ann. §46.035 (b)(1))

2. On premises of a correctional facility (Tex. Penal Code Ann. §46.035 (b)(3))

3. On the physical premises of a school or educational institution, any grounds or building on which an activity sponsored by a school or educational institution is being conducted, or a passenger transportation vehicle of a school or educational institution, whether the school or educational institution is public or private unless pursuant to written regulation or authorization. (Tex. Penal Code Ann. §46.03 (a)(1))

4. On the premises where a high school, collegiate or professional sporting event of interscholastic event is taking place, unless the license holder is a participant in the event and a handgun is used in the event. (Tex. Penal Code Ann. §46.035 (b)(2))

5. On the premises of a polling place on the day of an election or while early voting is in progress. (Tex. Penal Code Ann. §46.03 (a)(2))

6. Racetrack; (Tex. Penal Code Ann. §46.03 (a)(4))

7. Secured area of an airport (Tex. Penal Code Ann. §46.03 (a)(5))

8. In any government court or offices utilized by the court, unless pursuant to written regulations or written authorization of the court. Tex. Penal Code Ann. §46.03 (a)(3)

9. Within 1000 feet of a place of execution (When the circumstances set forth in Tex. Penal Code Ann. §46.03 (a)(6)(A) and (B) exist)

10. On the premises of a Hospital or nursing home licensed under the Health and Safety Code unless license holder has written authorization to carry. (Tex. Penal Code Ann. §46.035 (b)(4)) (*If Posted)

11. Amusement parks. (Tex. Penal Code Ann. §46.035 (b)(5)) (*If Posted)

    a. Amusement Parks means a permanent indoor or outdoor facility or park where amusement rides are available for use by the public that is located in a county with a population of more than one million, encompasses at least 75 acres in surface area, is enclosed with access only through controlled entries, is open for operation more than 120 days in each calendar year, and has security guards on the premises at all times. The term does not include any public or private driveway, street, sidewalk or walkway, parking lot, parking garage, or other parking area. (Tex. Penal Code Ann. §46.035 (f)(1))

12. On the premises of a civil commitment facility. Tex. Penal Code Ann. § 46.035 (b)(5)

13. Any public or private building (If posted, see "Posted Buildings" special note below)

14. Administrative Regulations prohibit carry in the following areas:

   a. **Assisted living facility** (Tex. Health & Safety Code Ann. §247.065(b)(9); 40 Tex. Admin. Code §92.125(b)(2)(I)). **Foster homes** (40 Tex. Admin. Code §48.8907(i)(6)). **The grounds of a horse racing association** (16 Tex. Admin. Code §311.211, 311.215); **Meetings of the Windham School District Board of Trustees** (19 Tex. Admin. Code §300.1(g); only handgun, not long gun, possession is prohibited); **Facilities offering or providing chemical dependency treatment services** (25 Tex. Admin. Code §448.505); State parks, if there is a cartridge or projectile in any portion of the mechanism, except when authorized by Commission on State Parks or its director (31 Tex. Admin. Code §59.134(f)); **Public hunting lands**, except by persons authorized by the Parks and Wildlife Department to hunt or conduct research on the area (31 Tex. Admin. Code §65.199(2); **State buildings or state grounds within the Capitol Complex**, except by a person licensed to carry a concealed handgun (37 Tex. Admin. Code §3.146(a)); **The premises of buildings, offices, facilities, or programs operated by or under contract with the Texas Youth Commission**, except in certain areas by a person licensed to carry a concealed handgun (37 Tex. Admin. Code §81.31, 97.1); **The premises of a juvenile justice alternative education program** (37 Tex. Admin. Code §348.10(j)); and **Child-care centers** (40 Tex. Admin. Code §746.3707(b)).

**Permits Recognized By This State:** Alabama, Alaska, Arizona, Arkansas, California, Colorado, Connecticut, Delaware, Florida, Georgia, Hawaii, Idaho, Indiana, Iowa, Kansas, Kentucky, Louisiana, Maryland, Massachusetts, Michigan, Mississippi, Missouri, Montana, Nebraska, Nevada, New Jersey, New Mexico, New York, North Carolina, North Dakota, Ohio, Oklahoma, Pennsylvania, Rhode Island, South Carolina, South Dakota, Tennessee, Utah, Virginia, Washington, West Virginia, Wyoming

## Special Notes:

**Police Encounters - Quasi Duty to Inform:** Texas has a **stronger than usual quasi duty to inform law**, which says that although you are not required to affirmatively inform an officer that you have a firearm, you must give the officer your concealed firearm permit when they ask to see your identification. This means in a standard traffic stop where you are asked to provide your photo ID, you will also have to provide the officer with your carry permit.

- **The Law:** If a license holder is carrying a handgun on or about the license holder's person when a magistrate or a peace officer demands that the license holder display identification, the license holder shall display both the

license holder's driver's license or identification certificate issued by the department and the license holder's handgun license.
Tex. Gov't Code Ann. § 411.205

**Posted Buildings:** Posted areas must be posted in accordance with the following language:

"PURSUANT TO SECTION 30.06, PENAL CODE (TRESPASS BY HOLDER OF A LICENSE TO CARRY A CONCEALED HANDGUN) A PERSON LICENSED UNDER SUBCHAPTER H, CHAPTER 411, GOVERNMENT CODE (CONCEALED HANDGUN LAW), MAY NOT ENTER THIS PROPERTY WITH A CONCEALED HANDGUN."

**Employers** cannot restrict an employee from storing a firearm in a locked private vehicle in a parking lot. 37 Tex. Admin. Code § 97.3.

**Colleges:** Permit holders may carry on four-year public colleges, universities, or community college campuses. The firearm must remain concealed, open carry is not permitted. Be aware schools are generally allowed to set their own rules regarding firearms, check with the school prior to carrying.

**Carrying a Firearm While Intoxicated:** §46.035, Texas Penal Code states that it is unlawful for an individual who is intoxicated to carry a handgun. It is important to note that the Penal Code defines "intoxicated" as not having the normal use of mental or physical faculties by reason of the introduction of alcohol, a controlled substance, a drug, a dangerous drug, a combination of two or more of those substances, or any other substance in the body; or having an alcohol concentration of .08 or more.

**Parking Lots**: "Thus, while section 46.035 prohibits the carrying of a handgun at the foregoing places, it does not prohibit the carrying of a handgun in the driveway, street, sidewalk or walkway, parking lot, parking garage..." Tex. Atty. Gen. Op., No. DM-363 (1995).

- A school district or open-enrollment charter school may not prohibit a person, including a school employee, who holds a license to carry a handgun from transporting or storing a handgun or other firearm or ammunition in a locked, privately owned or leased motor vehicle in a parking lot, parking garage, or other parking area provided by the district or charter school and may not regulate the manner in which the handgun, firearm, or ammunition is stored in the vehicle, provided that the handgun, firearm, or ammunition is not in plain view. Tex. Educ. Code Ann. § 37.0815

# Utah

*"The individual right of the people to keep and bear arms for security and defense of self, family, others, property, or the state, as well as for other lawful purposes shall not be infringed; but nothing herein shall prevent the legislature from defining the lawful use of arms."*

*Art. I, § 6*

**Rating:** ★ ★ ★ ★ ★

State of Utah
Department of Public Safety
P.O. Box 148280
Salt Lake City, UT 84114
(801) 965-4445

## Prohibited Areas

### Places Off Limits to Firearms Under State Law:

1. A house of worship, if the house of worship, 1: gives personal communication that firearms are prohibited, or 2: posts signs reasonably likely to come to the attention of persons entering the house of worship, or 3: publishing the weapons policy in a bulletin, newsletter, worship program, or similar document, or 4: formally registering as off limits to firearms with the State of Utah) (§76-10-530)

2. A private residence if notice is given by 1: personal communication that firearms are prohibited, or 2: posting of signs reasonably likely to come to the attention of persons entering the residence. (Utah Code Ann. § 76-10-530)

3. Secure areas* of mental health facilities (Utah Code Ann. §76-8-311.1(d))

4. Secure areas* of prison, correctional, or jail facilities (Utah Code Ann. §76-8-311.1(c))

5. Courthouses: Unless authorized by the rules of judicial administration, any person who knowingly or intentionally possesses a firearm, ammunition, or dangerous weapon within a secure area established by the judicial council under this section is guilty of a third degree felony. (Utah Code Ann. § 78A-2-203; Rules of Judicial Administration 3-414.)

6. Any areas dedicated secure by state law (Utah Code Ann. §53-5-710)

**Permits Recognized By This State: ALL STATE PERMITS**

**Special Notes:**

**Age to Obtain Permit:** Effective 05/07/17 anyone age 18-20 will be able to obtain a "provisional" concealed carry permit from Utah by taking the same training course as the standard Utah permit. This "provisional" permit will allow someone age 18-20 to carry in all the same places a standard Utah permit does, with the singular exception of a public or private primary or secondary school campus. see § 53-5-704.5

**Alcohol Limitation:** Any person who carries a dangerous weapon while under the influence of alcohol or a controlled substance is guilty of a class B misdemeanor. Prior to December 30, 2018 under the influence means .08. After December 30, 2018 Utah law will define under the influence as a breath alcohol concentration of .05 or greater. Utah Code Ann. § 76-10-528

**Firearms Allowed in Parking Lots:** A person may not establish, maintain, or enforce any policy or rule that has the effect of: (a) prohibiting any individual from transporting or storing a firearm in a motor vehicle on any property designated for motor vehicle parking, if:

- (i) the individual is legally permitted to transport, possess, purchase, receive, transfer, or store the firearm;

- (ii) the firearm is locked securely in the motor vehicle or in a locked container attached to the motor vehicle while the motor vehicle is not occupied; and

- (iii) the firearm is not in plain view from the outside of the motor vehicle. Utah Code Ann. § 34-45-103.

**Permitless Vehicle Carry of Handguns Allowed:** A person over the age of 18 may possess a loaded handgun in a vehicle without a permit so long as: (A) The person is not otherwise prohibited from possessing a firearm; and (B) The vehicle is in the person's lawful possession; or the person is carrying the loaded firearm in a vehicle with the consent of the person lawfully in possession of the vehicle; Utah Code Ann. § 76-10-505

**Posted "No Guns Allowed" Businesses:** In Utah businesses who prohibit carry via posting a "no guns allowed" sign do not have force of law to backup their policy. If a business asks you to leave you must do so or face criminal trespass charges, however the mere carrying of a firearm into a posted business does not constitute a crime in Utah.

**\*Secure Area Defined**: "Secure area" means any area into which certain persons are restricted from transporting any firearm, ammunition, dangerous weapon, or explosive. A "secure area" may not include any area normally accessible to the public. At least one notice shall be prominently displayed at each entrance to an area in which a firearm, ammunition, dangerous weapon, or explosive is restricted.Provisions shall be made to provide a secure weapons storage area so that persons entering the secure area may store their weapons prior to entering the secure area. The entity operating the facility shall be responsible for weapons while they are stored in the storage area. Utah Code Ann. § 76-8-311.1

# Vermont

*"That the people have a right to bear arms for the defense of themselves and the State -- and as standing armies in time of peace are dangerous to liberty, they ought not to be kept up; and that the military should be kept under strict subordination to and governed by the civil power."*

*Ch. I, art. 16*

**Rating:** ★ ★ ★ ★ ★

State of Vermont
Department of Public Safety
Criminal Justice Services
103 South Main Street
Waterbury, VT 05671
(802) 244-8786

## Prohibited Areas

### Places Off Limits to Firearms Under State Law:

1. Public and private schools and school busses (Vt. Stat. Ann. tit.13, §4004(a))

2. State institutions/Buildings (Vt. Stat. Ann. tit.29, §152(a)(14))

3. Courthouses (Vt. Stat. Ann. tit.13, §4106)

4. Secured buildings ("Secured building" means a building with controlled points of public access, metal screening devices at each point of public access, and locked compartments, accessible only to security personnel for storage of checked firearms)

5. State administrative regulations also govern firearms at:

    a. State-Owned Historic Sites - no "display" of firearms allowed (Vt. Code R. §11 050.002(II)(2.7)

    b. The Mud Creek Controlled Hunting Area (Vt. Code R. §12.010.019)

    c. Bomoseen State Game Refuge (10-119 V.T. Code R. § 5226)

    d. The premises of a legally exempt child care provider (Vt. Code R. §13.160.002)

    e. Residential child-care facilities (Vt. Code R. §13.162.006)

    f. Licensed foster homes (Vt. Code R. §13.162.007)

        i. Any firearm shall be kept in a locked storage space with ammunition stored separately in a locked space, or shall be incapacitated by means of the locking of essential parts of the firearm or the removal and separate locking of such parts.

    g. Limited Access Facilities of State Highways. (Vt. Code R. §14.053.004)

**Permits Recognized By This State:** N/A. Vermont allows all who can legally possess a firearm to carry a firearm in a concealed manner without a permit.

## Special Notes:

**Constitutional Carry:** Vermont holds that residents and non-residents are allowed to open carry or concealed carry without requiring a permit so long as the person in possession of the firearm is not otherwise prohibited from possessing it by state or federal law. Vt. Const. ch. I, art. 16

**State Parks:** No firearms may be discharged in any state park between the dates of May 1st and October 15th.

**Large Capacity Magazine Ban:** A person shall not manufacture, possess, transfer, offer for sale, purchase, or receive or import into this State a large capacity ammunition feeding device. The prohibition on possession, transfer, sale, and purchase of large capacity ammunition feeding devices shall not apply to a large capacity ammunition feeding device lawfully possessed on or before the effective date of this section (April 1, 2018).

- "large capacity ammunition feeding device" means a magazine, belt, drum, feed strip, or similar device that has a capacity of, or that can be readily restored or converted to accept:
  - (A) more than 10 rounds of ammunition for a long gun; or
  - (B) more than 15 rounds of ammunition for a hand gun.
- The term "large capacity ammunition feeding device" shall not include:
  - (A) an attached tubular device designed to accept, and capable of operating only with, .22 caliber rimfire ammunition;
  - (B) a large capacity ammunition feeding device that is manufactured or sold solely for use by a lever action or bolt action long gun or by an antique firearm as defined in subdivisions 4017(d)(2)(A) and (B) of this title;

Vt. Stat. Ann. tit. 13, § 4021

# Virginia

*"That a well regulated militia, composed of the body of the people, trained to arms, is the proper, natural, and safe defense of a free state, therefore, the right of the people to keep and bear arms shall not be infringed; that standing armies, in time of peace, should be avoided as dangerous to liberty; and that in all cases the military should be under strict subordination to, and governed by, the civil power."*

*Art. I, § 13*

**Rating:** ★ ★ ★ ★

Virginia State Police
P.O. Box 27472
Richmond, VA 23261
(804) 674-2000

## Prohibited Areas

### Places Off Limits to Firearms Under State Law:

1. No person who carries a concealed handgun onto the premises of any restaurant or club as defined in § 4.1-100 for which a license to sell and serve alcoholic beverages for on-premises consumption has been granted by the Virginia Alcoholic Beverage Control Board under Title 4.1 of the Code of Virginia may consume an alcoholic beverage while on the premises. (May carry into premises but MAY NOT drink). (Va. Code Ann. §18.2-308(J3))

2. Private property when prohibited by the owner of the property, or where posted as prohibited. (Va. Code Ann. §18.2-308(O))

3. To a place of worship while a meeting for religious purposes is being held at such place, without good and sufficient reason.   (See special notes) (Va. Code Ann. §18.2-283)

4. Courthouse. (Va. Code Ann. §18.2-283.1)

5. School property, including public, private, or religious preschools and licensed child day centers. Exceptions to this statute include a person who has a valid concealed handgun permit and possesses a concealed handgun while in a motor vehicle in a parking lot, traffic circle, or other means of vehicular ingress or egress to the school. (Va. Code Ann. §18.2-308.1)

6. Air carrier airport terminal. (Va. Code Ann. §18.2-287.01)

7. University property, in academic buildings, administrative office buildings, student residence buildings, dining facilities, or while attending sporting, entertainment or educational events. (8 Va. Admin. Code §35-60-20)

8. Regional Jail or Juvenile Detention Facility

9. Some Wildlife Management Areas (4 Va. Admin. Code §15-40-120)

**Permits Recognized By This State: ALL STATE PERMITS**

**Special Notes:**

**Warning! Poor Preemption -** Effective July 1, 2020 cities and localities can now adopt their own regulations prohibiting the possession or carrying of firearms in certain locations. Check with local ordinances as these may change often and may vary from city to city.

- **The Law:** A locality may adopt an ordinance that prohibits the possession, carrying, or transportation of any firearms, ammunition, or components or combination thereof (i) in any building, or part thereof, owned or used by such locality, or by any authority or local governmental entity created or controlled by the locality, for governmental purposes; (ii) in any public park owned or operated by the locality, or by any authority or local governmental entity created or controlled by the locality; (iii) in any recreation or community center facility operated by the locality, or by any authority or local governmental entity created or controlled by the locality; or (iv) in any public street, road, alley, or sidewalk or public right-of-way or any other place of whatever nature that is open to the public and is being used by or is adjacent to a permitted event or an event that would otherwise require a permit. In buildings that are not owned by a locality, or by any authority or local governmental entity created or controlled by the locality, such ordinance shall apply only to the part of the building that is being used for a governmental purpose and when such building, or part thereof, is being used for a governmental purpose. Va. Code Ann. § 15.2-915

**Open Carry Prohibited in Government Buildings:** Executive Order Number 50 (2015) states, in part, "*I hereby declare that it is the policy of the Commonwealth that open carry of firearms shall be prohibited in offices occupied by executive branch agencies, unless held by law enforcement, authorized security, or military personnel authorized to carry firearms in accordance with their duties.*"

**Age to Carry:** It shall be unlawful for any person under 18 years of age to knowingly and intentionally possess or transport a handgun or assault firearm anywhere in the Commonwealth. (Va. Code Ann. § 18.2-308.7)

**Places Of Worship:** Virginia Attorney General Ken Cuccinelli II has published an opinion stating that while it is unlawful under Virginia law to possess firearms in a place of worship or religious meeting absent "good and sufficient reason," in his opinion, "carrying a weapon for personal protection constitutes a good and sufficient reason under the statute." (Opinion No. 11-043 – April 2011)

# Washington

*"The right of the individual citizen to bear arms in defense of himself, or the state, shall not be impaired, but nothing in this section shall be construed as authorizing individuals or corporations to organize, maintain or employ an armed body of men."*

Art. I, § 24

**Rating:** ★ ★ ★

State of Washington
Office of the Attorney General
Licensing & Employment
Security Division
P.O. Box 40110
Olympia, WA 98504
(360) 753-2702

## Prohibited Areas

**Places Off Limits to Firearms Under State Law:**

1.  The restricted access areas of a jail, or of a law enforcement facility, or any place used for the confinement of a person. (Restricted access areas do not include common areas of egress or ingress open to the general public) (Wash Rev. Code §9.41.300)

2.  Public or private elementary or secondary school premises, school-provided transportation, or areas of facilities while being used exclusively by public or private schools" (Wash Rev. Code §9.41.280)

    a.  This prohibition does not apply to: (e) Any person in possession of a pistol who has been issued a license under Wash Rev. Code §9.41.070 **while picking up or dropping off a student**; (f) Any non-student at least eighteen years of age legally in possession of a firearm or dangerous weapon that is secured within an attended vehicle or concealed from view within a locked unattended vehicle while conducting legitimate business at the school. )Wash. Rev. Code §9.41.280)

3.  Those areas in any building which are used in connection with court proceedings, including courtrooms, jury rooms, judge's chambers, offices and areas used to conduct court business, waiting areas, and corridors adjacent to areas used in connection with court proceedings. (Wash Rev. Code §9.41.300)

4.  The restricted access areas of a public mental health facility certified by the department of social and health services for inpatient hospital care and state institutions for the care of the mentally ill, excluding those facilities solely for evaluation and treatment. (Wash Rev. Code §9.41.300)

5.  That portion of an establishment classified by the state liquor control board as off-limits to persons under twenty-one years of age; (Wash Rev. Code §9.41.300)

6.  The restricted access areas of a commercial service airport designated in the airport security plan approved by the federal transportation security administration, including passenger screening checkpoints at or beyond the point at which a passenger initiates the screening process. (Any restricted access area shall be clearly indicated by prominent signs indicating that firearms and other weapons are prohibited in the area).

7. Outdoor music festivals. (Wash Rev. Code §70.108.150)

8. All facilities owned, leased, or operated by the office of administrative hearings and in rooms where the office of administrative hearings is conducting an administrative hearing. (Wash. Admin. Code §10-20-010(1))

9. Licensed child care center premises, child care center-provided transportation, or areas of facilities while being used exclusively by a child care center. This prohibition does not apply to any person in possession of a pistol who has been issued a license, while picking up or dropping off a child at the child care center. Wash. Rev. Code Ann. § 9.41.0003.

10. Washington State Administrative Rules prohibit firearms in at least the following locations: Colleges or Universities; Racing Grounds; Wash.Admin. Code 110-305-4725; 110-145-1660; 260-20-075

**Permits Recognized By This State:** Arkansas, Idaho (Enhanced Permit Only), Kansas, Louisiana, Michigan, Mississippi, North Carolina, North Dakota (class one permits only), Ohio, Oklahoma, South Dakota (enhanced permits only), Tennessee, Utah (Non-resident permits recognized only for holders 21 and older)

## Special Notes:

**Police Encounters - Quasi Duty to Inform:** Washington is a **quasi duty to inform** state, which means that you are not affirmatively required to tell a police officer that you have a firearm in your possession, but if you are asked by an officer during a lawful stop you must provide them with your permit.

- **The Law**: Every licensee shall have his or her concealed pistol license in his or her immediate possession at all times that he or she is required by this section to have a concealed pistol license and shall display the same upon demand to any police officer or to any other person when and if required by law to do so. (Wash Rev. Code §9.41.050 )

**Vehicle Carry:** A person shall not carry or place a loaded pistol in any vehicle unless the person has a license to carry a concealed pistol and: (i) The pistol is on the licensee's person, (ii) the licensee is within the vehicle at all times that the pistol is there, or (iii) the licensee is away from the vehicle and the pistol is locked within the vehicle and concealed from view from outside the vehicle. Wash. Rev. Code Ann. § 9.41.050

**Possession of a handgun by someone 18-21:** Unless an exception under Wash Rev. Code §9.41.042, §9.41.050, or §9.41.060 applies, a person at least eighteen years of age, but less than twenty-one years of age, may possess a pistol only:(1) In the person's place of abode;(2) At the person's fixed place of business; or (3) On real property under his or her control.

**Outdoor Music Festivals:** "Outdoor music festival" or "music festival" or "festival" means an assembly of persons gathered primarily for outdoor, live or recorded musical entertainment, where the predicted attendance is two thousand persons or more and where the duration of the program is five hours or longer. Wash. Rev. Code Ann. § 70.108.020.

# Washington D.C.

*The District of Columbia has NO provision for the right to keep and bear arms.*

**Rating:** ★

Office of the Attorney General
441 4th Street, NW, Suite 1145S
Washington, DC 20001
(202) 727-3400

## Prohibited Areas

### Places Off Limits to Firearms Under State Law:

**No person holding a license shall carry a pistol in the following locations or under the following circumstances: (see D.C. Code Ann. § 7-2509.07)**

1. A building or office occupied by the District of Columbia or its agencies.

2. The building and grounds, including any adjacent parking lot or a childcare facility, preschool, elementary or secondary school, or a public or private college or university.

3. A hospital or an office where medical or mental health services are the primary services provided.

4. A penal institution, secure juvenile residential facility, or halfway house.

5. A polling place while voting is occurring.

6. A public transportation vehicle, including the Metro-rail transit system and its stations.

7. Any premises where alcohol is served, sold and consumed on the premises (pursuant to license issued under Title 25 of D.C. Code)

8. Stadium or Arena

9. Public Gathering or special event open to the public when the organizer has provided notice and posted signage prohibiting the carrying of pistols in advance of the gathering or special event.

10. The public memorials on the National Mall and along the Tidal Basin, and any area where firearms are prohibited under federal law or by a federal agency, including the U.S. Capitol buildings and grounds.

11. The area around the White House (between Constitution Ave. and H St. and between 15th St. and 17th St. NW)

12. The U.S. Naval Observatory and its grounds (from the perimeter of its fence to the curb of Massachusetts Ave. NW from 34th St. south on Massachusetts Ave to Observatory Circle NW)

13. When a dignitary or high-ranking official of the United States or a state, local, or foreign government is moving under the protection of the MPD, the U.S Secret Service, the U.S Capitol Police, or other law enforcement agency that does not include a distance greater than 1,000 feet from the moving dignitary. ( provided notice has been given by signs or an officer's order)

14. A Demonstration in a public place (within a perimeter of 1,000 feet designated by a law enforcement agency, and notice has been given by signs or an officer's order)

15. On private residential property unless authorized by the property owner.

16. A place of religious worship unless authorized by the owner or authorized agent.

17. Non-residential property that is posted with conspicuous signage prohibiting the carrying of a concealed pistol.

**Whenever a licensee carries a concealed pistol and approaches any prohibited location, or is subject to any prohibited circumstance, the licensee shall:**

1. If the licensee is in a vehicle or if a vehicle is readily available, immediately secure the pistol in the manner prescribed in section 4b(b) of An Act To control the possession, sale, transfer, and use of pistols and other dangerous weapons in the District of Columbia, to provide penalties, to prescribe rules of evidence, and for other purposes, effective May 20, 2009 (D.C. Law 17-388; D.C. Official Code § 22-4504.02(b)); or

2. If the licensee does not have a vehicle available, immediately leave the prohibited location or circumstance.

**A licensee shall not be in violation of this section:**

1. While he or she is traveling along any public street, road, or highway (including any adjacent public sidewalk) that touches the perimeter of any of the premises under subsection (a) of this section or that are prohibited under subsection (b) of this section if the concealed pistol is carried on his or her person in accordance with this act, or is being transported by the licensee in accordance with section 4b of An Act To control the possession, sale, transfer, and use of pistols and other dangerous weapons in the District of Columbia, to provide penalties, to prescribe rules of evidence, and for other purposes, effective May 20, 2009 (D.C. Law 17-388; D.C. Official Code § 22-4504.02);

**Permits Recognized By This State: NONE**

## Special Notes:

**Police Encounters - Duty to Inform:** Washington DC is **a duty to inform jurisdiction,** which means that you must immediately inform an officer of the presence of a concealed firearm when approached or addressed by and officer, and you must display your permit and identification upon request from the officer.

- **The Law:** A licensee shall have on or about his or her person each time the pistol is carried in the District:

    1. The license; and

    2. The registration certificate for the pistol being carried, issued pursuant to this unit.

If a law enforcement officer initiates an investigative stop of a licensee carrying a concealed pistol or with someone who is with the stopped licensee at the time of the investigative stop, shall:

    1. Disclose to the officer that he or she is carrying a concealed pistol;

    2. Present the license and registration certificate;

    3. Identify the location of the concealed pistol; and

    4. Comply with all lawful orders and directions from the officer, including allowing a pat down of his or her person and permitting the law enforcement officer to take possession of the pistol for so long as is necessary for the safety of the officer or the public.

D.C. Code Ann. § 7-2509.04

**Alcohol:** A licensee may not carry a pistol while impaired...For the purposes of this section, the term "impaired" means a licensee has consumed alcohol or a drug or a combination thereof and that it has affected the licensee's behavior in a way that can be perceived or noticed. 2013 Washington DC Legislative Bill No. 927, Washington DC Council Period Twenty, 2013 Washington DC Legislative Bill No. 927, Washington DC Council Period Twenty

**Large Capacity Magazine:** DC has banned the possession, sell, or transfer of any large capacity magazine, and defines large capacity as holding 10+ rounds of ammunition. (D.C. Official Code §7-2506.01).

# West Virginia

*"A person has the right to keep and bear arms for the defense of self, family, home and state, and for lawful hunting and recreational use."*

Art. III, § 22

**Rating:** ★ ★ ★ ★

State of West Virginia
State Police Headquarters
725 Jefferson Road South
Charleston, WV 25309
(305) 746-2100

## Prohibited Areas

### Places Off Limits to Firearms Under State Law:

1. Magistrates Office (W. Va. Code §61-7-11a)

2. Primary and Secondary School Property including School buses (W. Va. Code §61-7-11a)

3. Any facility that is being used for a Primary or Secondary School function while that function is going on (W. Va. Code §61-7-11a)

4. Vocational Education Building (W. Va. Code §61-7-11a)

5. Courthouses (W. Va. Code §61-7-11a)

6. Family Law Masters office (W. Va. Code §61-7-11a)

7. Anywhere a sign is posted saying no Firearms Allowed. (These signs do not have to be of any set size or design). (W. Va. Code §61-7-11a)

8. Regional jails, detention facilities or State Division of Corrections facilities and their grounds.

9. Private Property (If asked to leave): Any person carrying or possessing a firearm or other deadly weapon on the property of another who refuses to temporarily relinquish possession of such firearm or other deadly weapon, upon being requested to do so, or to leave such premises, while in possession of such firearm or other deadly weapon, shall be guilty of a misdemeanor, and, upon conviction thereof, shall be fined not more than one thousand dollars or confined in the county jail not more than six months. W. Va. Code Ann. § 61-7-14.

10. Law enforcement facilities (W. Va. Code §61-7-11a)

11. State Capitol buildings (W. Va. Code §61-6-19)

12. Child care centers (W. Va. Code §78-01-20.3.a)

13. State homes for veterans (W. Va. Code §86-1-5.3.g)

14. Domestic violence shelters (W. Va. Code §191-2-5.1.b)

15. West Virginia has a unique grandfather law for municipalities, the following municipality restrictions are in effect within their jurisdiction. These are IN ADDITION to the above mentioned state areas and subject to change:

16. Charleston WV Prohibited Areas: (§78-165)

    a. City hall,

    b. Municipal auditorium,

    c. The civic center,

    d. All parks and recreation buildings and facilities, including recreation centers, playgrounds, swimming pools, dressing areas, tennis courts, parks and recreation areas and all other buildings, structures, facilities, and grounds thereof, owned or occupied by the City of Charleston; however, the provisions of this section shall not apply to city, county, sate and federal law enforcement officers and to exhibitors and performers at city-sanctioned events who obtain advance written authorization from the chief of police. (Ord. No. 4941, 4-19-1993; Bill No. 7103, 12-6-2004)

17. Dunbar WV Prohibited Areas: (§545.13)

    a. Dunbar City Hall.

    b. Any City municipal building or any City owned park.

    c. A sign shall be posted at Dunbar City Hall and other municipal buildings and parks

18. South Charleston, WV Prohibited Areas: (§545.15)

    a. Any City-owned building, park or recreation area

**Permits Recognized By This State:** Alabama, Alaska, Arizona, Arkansas, Colorado, Delaware, Florida, Georgia, Idaho, Indiana, Iowa, Kansas, Kentucky, Ohio, Oklahoma, Pennsylvania, Louisiana, Michigan, Mississippi, Missouri, Montana, Nevada, New Hampshire, New Mexico, North Carolina, North Dakota, South Carolina, South Dakota, Tennessee, Texas, Utah, Virginia, Wisconsin, Wyoming **Note: Non-resident permits recognized only for holders age 21 and older**

**Special Notes:**

**Constitutional Carry:** Effective June 5, 2016 any person may carry a concealed deadly weapon in West Virginia without a license so long as they are:

- At least twenty-one years of age; A United States citizen or legal resident thereof; Not prohibited from possessing a firearm under the provisions of this section; and Not prohibited from possessing a firearm under the provisions W. Va. Code Ann. § 61-7-7

**School Zone Vehicle Exception:** It is not illegal, while on school property, to have an unloaded firearm or deadly weapon locked in a motor vehicle W. Va. Code Ann. § 61-7-11a

# Wisconsin

*"The people have the right to keep and bear arms for security, defense, hunting, recreation or any other lawful purpose."*

*Art. I, § 25*

**Rating:** ★ ★ ★ ★

State of Wisconsin
Department of Justice
Crime Information Bureau
P.O. Box 2718
Madison, WI 53701
(608) 266-7314

## Prohibited Areas

**Places Off Limits to Firearms Under State Law:**

1. Any portion of a building that is a police station, sheriff's office, state patrol station, or the office of a division of criminal investigation special agent of the department (Wis. Stat. §176.60(16))

2. Any portion of a building that is a prison, jail, house of correction, or secured correctional facility (Wis. Stat. §176.60(16))

3. The Sand Ridge Secure Treatment Center, the Wisconsin Resource Center, or any secured unit or secured portion of a mental health institution, including a facility designated as the Maximum Security Facility at the Mendota Mental Health Institute.

4. Any secured unit or secured portion of a mental health institute under s. 51.05, including a facility designated as the Maximum Security Facility at Mendota Mental Health Institute. (Wis. Stat. §176.60(16))

5. Any portion of a building that is a county, state, or federal courthouse (Wis. Stat. §176.60(16))

6. Any portion of a building that is a municipal courtroom if court is in session (Wis. Stat. §176.60(16))

7. Any individual who knowingly possesses a firearm at a place that the individual knows, or has reasonable cause to believe, is in or on the grounds of a school is guilty of a Class I felony. **A person who is a CCW licensee or out-of-state CCW licensee may possess a firearm within 1,000 feet of the grounds of a school, but not in or on school grounds**. (Wis. Stat. § 948.605(2)(b)1r)

8. A posted building (including government buildings, special events, & universities) that have orally informed you of their policy prohibiting firearms or that post a sign at least 11 inches square is placed in at least 2 conspicuous places (Wis. Stat. §943(13))

9. A place beyond a security checkpoint in an airport (Wis. Stat. §176.60(16))

10. Persons who do not have a CCW permit may not carry a handgun in a tavern and those persons with a CCW license **may carry a concealed handgun in a tavern only if NOT consuming alcohol**. (Wis. Stat. § 941.237(3)(cx))

The prohibitions above (**excluding #7**) do not apply to any of the following:

1. A weapon in a vehicle driven or parked in a parking facility located in a building that is used as, or any portion of which is used as, a location of the above prohibited areas (excluding #7).

2. A weapon in a courthouse or courtroom if a judge who is a licensee is carrying the weapon or if another licensee or out-of-state licensee, whom a judge has permitted in writing to carry a weapon, is carrying the weapon.

3. A weapon in a courthouse or courtroom if a district attorney, or an assistant district attorney, who is a licensee is carrying the weapon.

**Permits Recognized By This State:** Alabama, Alaska, Arizona, Arkansas, California, Colorado, Connecticut, Delaware,  Florida, Georgia, Hawaii, Idaho, Illinois, Iowa, Kansas, Kentucky, Louisiana, Maryland, Massachusetts (Class A Licenses only), Michigan, Minnesota, Mississippi, Missouri, Montana, Nebraska, Nevada, New Mexico, New York, North Carolina, North Dakota,  Oklahoma (if issued or renewed after 10/01/18), Pennsylvania, Puerto Rico, Rhode Island, South Carolina, South Dakota (Enhanced Permit Only), Tennessee, Texas, U.S Virgin Islands, Utah, Virginia (non-resident VA permits only), Washington, Washington DC, West Virginia, Wyoming.

Note: Non-resident permits recognized only for holders age 21 and older

## Special Notes:

**Statewide Preemption:** On 03-09-17 the Wisconsin Supreme Court issued a ruling upholding Wisconsin's statewide firearm preemption law, which prohibits cities from enacting any firearm restrictions that go beyond state law. In this particular case the city of Madison had attempted to ban firearms on city buses, even when carried by permit holders. The court ruled Madison's ban was invalid.

## Wyoming

*"The right of citizens to bear arms in defense of themselves and of the state shall not be denied"*

*Art. I, § 24*

Office of the Attorney General
Division of Criminal
Investigation
316 West 22nd Street
Cheyenne, WY 82002

**Rating:** ★ ★ ★ ★

## Prohibited Areas

**Places Off Limits to Firearms Under State Law:**

1. Any facility used primarily for law enforcement operations or administration without the written consent of the chief administrator (Wyo. Stat. Ann. §6-8-104(t)(i))

2. Any detention facility, prison or jail (Wyo. Stat. Ann. §6-8-104(t)(ii))

3. Any courtroom, except that nothing in this section shall preclude a judge from carrying a concealed weapon or determining who will carry a concealed weapon in the courtroom (Wyo. Stat. Ann. §6-8-104(t)(iii))

4. Any meeting of a governmental entity (Wyo. Stat. Ann. §6-8-104(t)(iv))

5. Any meeting of the legislature or a committee thereof (Wyo. Stat. Ann. §6-8-104(t)(v))

6. Any school, college or professional athletic event not related to firearms (Wyo. Stat. Ann. §6-8-104(t)(vi))

7. Any portion of an establishment licensed to dispense alcoholic liquor and malt beverages for consumption on the premises, which portion of the establishment is primarily devoted to that purpose (Wyo. Stat. Ann. §6-8-104(t)(vii))

8. Any place where persons are assembled for public worship, without the written consent of the chief administrator of that place (Wyo. Stat. Ann. §6-8-104(t)(viii))

9. Any elementary or secondary school facility (Wyo. Stat. Ann. §6-8-104(t)(ix))

10. Any college or university facility without the written consent of the security service of the college or university (Wyo. Stat. Ann. §6-8-104(t)(x))

11. State Capitol Building or building under the jurisdiction of SBC (WY ADC BC Gen Ch. 6§2)

12. Posted Property: A person is guilty of criminal trespass if he enters or remains on or in the land or premises of another person, knowing he is not authorized to do so, or after being notified to depart or to not trespass. For purposes of this section, notice is given by:

    a. Personal communication to the person by the owner or occupant, or his agent, or by a peace officer; or

    b. Posting of signs reasonably likely to come to the attention of intruders. Wyo. Stat. Ann. § 6-3-303

**Permits Recognized By This State:** Alabama, Alaska, Arizona, Arkansas, Colorado, Florida, Georgia, Idaho, Indiana, Iowa, Kansas, Kentucky, Louisiana, Maine, Michigan, Mississippi, Montana, Missouri, Nebraska, New Hampshire, Nevada, New Mexico, North Carolina, North Dakota, Ohio, Oklahoma, Pennsylvania, South Carolina, South Dakota, Tennessee, Texas, Utah, West Virginia, Wisconsin.

## Special Notes:

**Other Weapons Prohibited:** In Wyoming a permittee is only allowed to carry a concealed handgun; other weapons are not covered by the same protections.

**Constitutional Carry/Permitless Carry:** Effective July 1, 2011, Wyoming removed the requirement for **residents** to obtain or have a concealed firearm permit to carry a concealed firearm in the places allowed under state law, provided that the individual is at least 21 years of age and that the individual is not prohibited from possessing firearms by state or federal law. However, non-Wyoming residents must have a permit that is recognized by Wyoming in order to carry concealed there. [2011 SF 47 – amends W.S. 6-8-104(a)(iv)]

# Draw Your Own Reciprocity Map
Color in each state to match your current reciprocity map.

Permit Honored

Permit Not Honored

Permit Only Honored if
Held by Resident of
Issuing State

# State Attorney General Contact Information

| | |
|---|---|
| Alabama Attorney General | (334) 242-7300 |
| Alaska Attorney General | (907) 465-3600 |
| Arizona Attorney General | (602) 542-4266 |
| Arkansas Attorney General | (800) 482-8982 |
| California Attorney General | (916) 445-9555 |
| Colorado Attorney General | (303) 866-4500 |
| Connecticut Attorney General | (860) 808-5318 |
| Delaware Attorney General | (302) 577-8338 |
| Florida Attorney General | (850) 414-3300 |
| Georgia Attorney General | (404) 656-3300 |
| Hawaii Attorney General | (808) 586-1500 |
| Idaho Attorney General | (208) 334-2400 |
| Illinois Attorney General | (312) 814-3000 |
| Indiana Attorney General | (317) 232-6201 |
| Iowa Attorney General | (515) 281-5164 |
| Kansas Attorney General | (785) 296-2215 |
| Kentucky Attorney General | (502) 696-5300 |
| Louisiana Attorney General | (225) 326-6000 |
| Maine Attorney General | (207) 626-8800 |
| Maryland Attorney General | (410) 576-6300 |
| Massachusetts Attorney General | (617) 727-2200 |
| Michigan Attorney General | (517) 373-1110 |
| Minnesota Attorney General | (651) 296-3353 |
| Mississippi Attorney General | (601) 359-3680 |
| Missouri Attorney General | (573) 751-3321 |
| Montana Attorney General | (406) 444-2026 |
| Nebraska Attorney General | (402) 471-2682 |

| | |
|---|---|
| Nevada Attorney General | (775) 684-1100 |
| New Hampshire Attorney General | (603) 271-3658 |
| New Jersey Attorney General | (609) 292-8740 |
| New Mexico Attorney General | (505) 827-6000 |
| New York Attorney General | (518) 474-7330 |
| North Carolina Attorney General | (919) 716-6400 |
| North Dakota Attorney General | (701) 328-2210 |
| Ohio Attorney General | (614) 466-4320 |
| Oklahoma Attorney General | (405) 521-3921 |
| Oregon Attorney General | (503) 378-4732 |
| Pennsylvania Attorney General | (717) 787-3391 |
| Rhode Island Attorney General | (401) 274-4400 |
| South Carolina Attorney General | (803) 734-3970 |
| South Dakota Attorney General | (605) 773-3215 |
| Tennessee Attorney General | (615) 741-5860 |
| Texas Attorney General | (512) 463-2100 |
| Utah Attorney General | (801) 538-9600 |
| Vermont Attorney General | (802) 828-3173 |
| Virginia Attorney General | (804) 786-2071 |
| Washington Attorney General | (360) 753-6200 |
| Washington (District of Columbia) | (202) 724-1305 |
| West Virginia Attorney General | (304) 558-2021 |
| Wisconsin Attorney General | (608) 266-1221 |
| Wyoming Attorney General | (307) 777-7841 |

# 50 State NFA Weapon Law Summaries

In the United States there are two distinct classes of weapons, Title I and Title II. Title I weapons include standard rifles, handguns and shotguns. Title II weapons are those classified under Title II of the 1968 Gun Control Act, and include machine guns, silencers, short-barreled rifles and short barreled shotguns (among others). Acquisition of Title II weapons is legal in most states but requires federal approval from the Attorney General (through an application to the ATF), federal registration, payment of a $5 or $200 federal tax stamp fee, and sometimes state registration or permit fees. This quick check guide is designed to provide the readers with an overview of each state's laws regarding NFA (or Title II) weapons. The reader should consult with a qualified firearm law attorney in their home state regarding the process for acquiring one of these weapons.

## NFA Weapon Law Summaries include:

| State | Machine Gun or Silencer Ownership Allowed? | State Permit/ Registration Required? | Statute |
|---|---|---|---|
| ALABAMA | Machine Guns: Yes Silencers: Yes | No | No applicable statutes |
| ALASKA | Machine Guns: Yes Silencers: Yes | No | Alaska Stat. § 11.61.200(c) |
| ARIZONA | Machine Guns: Yes Silencers: Yes | No | Ariz. Rev. Stat. §§ 13-3101(A)(8)(iii), (B), 13-3102(A)(3) |
| ARKANSAS | Machine Guns: No Silencers: Yes | Machine Guns must be owned by a corporation for testing of ammunition or otherwise "under circumstances negating any likelihood that the weapon could be used as a weapon." | Ark. Code Ann. § 5-73-205 |

| State | Machine Gun or Silencer Ownership Allowed? | State Permit/ Registration Required? | Statute |
|-------|---------------------------------------------|--------------------------------------|---------|
| CALIFORNIA | Machine Guns: Yes<br>Silencers: No | Yes, permit required for machine guns | Cal. Penal Code § 32625(a); Cal. Penal Code § 32650 |
| COLORADO | Machine Guns: Yes<br>Silencers: Yes | Permit required for machine guns. | Colo. Rev. Stat. § 18-12-102(5) |
| CONNECTICUT | Machine Guns: Yes<br>Silencers: Yes | Registration is required for machine guns. | Conn. Gen. Stat. Ann. § 53-202 (g) |
| DELAWARE | Machine Guns: No<br>Silencers: No | Prohibited except for "persons possessing machine guns for scientific or experimental research and development purposes, which machine guns have been duly registered under the National Firearms Act of 1968" | Del. Code Ann. tit. 11, § 1444 |
| FLORIDA | Machine Guns: Yes<br>Silencers: Yes | No | Fla. Stat. Ann. § 790.221 |
| GEORGIA | Machine Guns: Yes<br>Silencers: Yes | No | Ga. Code Ann. § 16-11-124 (4) |
| HAWAII | Machine Guns: Yes<br>Silencers: No | Registration and permits are required for machine gun transfers post July 1994. | Haw. Rev. Stat. Ann. § 134-3<br><br>SBRs, SBSs also prohibited |

| State | Machine Gun or Silencer Ownership Allowed? | State Permit/ Registration Required? | Statute |
|---|---|---|---|
| IDAHO | Machine Guns: Yes Silencers: Yes | No | No applicable statutes |
| ILLINOIS | Machine Guns: No Silencers: No | Prohibited | 720 Ill. Comp. Stat. 5/24-1(a)(7)(i) SBRs, SBSs, DDs also prohibited |
| INDIANA | Machine Guns: Yes Silencers: Yes | No | Ind. Code Ann. § 35-47-5-10 (7) |
| IOWA | Machine Guns: No Silencers: Yes | Machine guns are prohibited. | Iowa Code §724.1(7) |
| KANSAS | Machine Guns: Yes Silencers: Yes | No | Kan. Stat. Ann. § 21-6301 (h) |
| KENTUCKY | Machine Guns: Yes Silencers: Yes | No | No applicable statutes |
| LOUISIANA | Machine Guns: No Silencers: Yes | Machine guns prohibited | La. Stat. Ann. § 40:1752 |
| MAINE | Machine Guns: Yes Silencers: Yes | No | Me. Rev. Stat. tit. 17-A, § 1052 |
| MARYLAND | Machine Guns: Yes Silencers: Yes | Registration required for Machine Guns. | Md. Code Ann., Crim. Law § 4-403(c)(1) |
| MASSACHUSETTS | Machine Guns: Yes, but restricted to "bona fide collectors" Silencers: Yes | Yes, license to possess required for Machine Guns. | Mass. Gen. Laws Ann. ch. 140, § 131 (o) Definition of "bona fide collector" 501 Mass. Code Regs. 6.02 |

| State | Machine Gun or Silencer Ownership Allowed? | State Permit/ Registration Required? | Statute |
|-------|---------------------------------------------|--------------------------------------|---------|
| MICHIGAN | Machine Guns: Yes<br>Silencers: Yes | No | Mich. Comp. Laws Serv. § 750.224(3) |
| MINNESOTA | Machine Guns: No, unless "primarily collector's items."<br>Silencers: Yes | Prohibited | Minn. Stat. § 609.67, subd. 3 |
| MISSISSIPPI | Machine Guns: Yes<br>Silencers: Yes | No | No applicable statutes |
| MISSOURI | Machine Guns: Yes<br>Silencers: Yes | No | Mo. Ann. Stat. § 571.020 (6) |
| MONTANA | Machine Guns: Yes<br>Silencers: Yes | No | Mont. Code Ann. § 45-8-305 |
| NEBRASKA | Machine Guns: Yes<br>Silencers: Yes | No | Neb. Rev. Stat. § 28-1203(2) |
| NEVADA | Machine Guns: Yes<br>Silencers: Yes | No | Nev. Rev. Stat. Ann. § 202.350(1)(b) |
| NEW HAMPSHIRE | Machine Guns: Yes<br>Silencers: Yes | No | |
| NEW JERSEY | Machine Guns: Yes, but restricted<br>Silencers: No | Yes, annual license required | N.J. Stat. Ann. § 2C:58-5 |
| NEW MEXICO | Machine Guns: Yes<br>Silencers: Yes | No | No applicable statutes |
| NEW YORK | Machine Guns: No<br>Silencers: No | Prohibited | N.Y. Penal Law §§ 265.02(2) |
| NORTH CAROLINA | Machine Guns: Yes<br>Silencers: Yes | No | N.C. Gen. Stat. § 14-409(b) |
| NORTH DAKOTA | Machine Guns: Yes<br>Silencers: Yes | No | N.D. Cent. Code § 62.1-05-01 |

| State | Machine Gun or Silencer Ownership Allowed? | State Permit/ Registration Required? | Statute |
|---|---|---|---|
| OHIO | Machine Guns: Yes, but restricted Silencers: Yes | Yes, license or temporary permit for dangerous ordnance required for Machine Guns. | Ohio Rev. Code Ann. § 2923.18 (A)(5) |
| OKLAHOMA | Machine Guns: Yes Silencers: Yes | No | No applicable statutes |
| OREGON | Machine Guns: Yes Silencers: Yes | No | Or. Rev. Stat. § 166.272 |
| PENNSYLVANIA | Machine Guns: Yes Silencers: Yes | No | 18 Pa. Cons. Stat. Ann. § 908(a) |
| RHODE ISLAND | Machine Guns: No Silencers: No | Prohibited | 11 R.I. Gen. Laws Ann. § 11-47-8 SBRs, SBSs also prohibited |
| SOUTH CAROLINA | Machine Guns: Yes Silencers: Yes | No | S.C. Code Ann. § 16-23-250 |
| SOUTH DAKOTA | Machine Guns: Yes Silencers: Yes | No | S.D. Codified Laws § 22-14-6(2) |
| TENNESSEE | Machine Guns: Yes Silencers: Yes | No | Tenn. Code Ann. § 39-17-1302 |
| TEXAS | Machine Guns: Yes Silencers: Yes | No | Tex. Penal Code § 46.05(b) |
| UTAH | Machine Guns: Yes Silencers: Yes | No | Utah Code Ann. § 76-10-509.4 |

| State | Machine Gun or Silencer Ownership Allowed? | State Permit/ Registration Required? | Statute |
|---|---|---|---|
| VERMONT | Machine Guns: Yes<br>Silencers: Yes | No | Vt. Stat. Ann. tit. 10, § 4704 prohibits use of machine gun or gun suppressor for hunting. |
| VIRGINIA | Machine Guns: Yes<br>Silencers: Yes | Yes, registration required | Va. Code Ann. § 18.2-295<br>Va. Code Ann. § 18.2-293.1. |
| WASHINGTON | Machine Guns: Restricted to those acquired prior to July 1, 1994<br>Silencers: Yes | Yes | Wash. Rev. Code Ann. § 9.41.190(4) |
| WEST VIRGINIA | Machine Guns: Yes<br>Silencers: Yes | No | W. Va. Code § 61-7-9 |
| WISCONSIN | Machine Guns: No<br>Silencers: Yes | Prohibited | Wis. Stat. § 941.26(1)(a) |
| WYOMING | Machine Guns: Yes<br>Silencers: Yes | No | Wyo. Stat. § 23-3-112 (a) prohibits hunting with a machine gun |
| DISTRICT OF COLUMBIA | Machine Guns: No<br>Silencers: No | Prohibited | D.C. Code Ann. § 7-2502.02(a)(2)<br>D.C. Code Ann. § 22-4514(a) |

# Duty To Retreat Law Summaries

In the criminal law system a duty to retreat is a duty that is sometimes imposed upon a citizen prior to the lawful use of deadly force in a self-defense situation. If applicable, it applies to the victim of unlawful force prior to their ability to use deadly force to defend him or herself. Generally speaking, if a state imposes a duty to retreat on an individual, such individual is only required to make reasonable efforts to retreat from unlawful force if they can do so in complete safety. Meaning, if there is a reasonable doubt that you cannot retreat without placing yourself, or a third party, in greater harm, then you have no duty to retreat from the force. You can stand your ground and meet force with force.

Nearly every state has codified duty to retreat laws, and they vary greatly. We have included concise summaries of the duty to retreat laws for each state to help supplement the average traveler. If you plan on staying in any particular state for any extended period of time, we advise you to consult an attorney to ensure that you know and understand any applicable laws and exceptions.

## Duty to Retreat Summaries

| State | Duty to Retreat |
|---|---|
| Alabama | No. A person who is otherwise justified in using deadly force (under §13A-3-23(a)), and who is not engaged in an unlawful activity and in any place where he or she has the right to be has no duty to retreat and has the right to stand his or her ground.  §13A-3-23(b) |
| Alaska | Yes, unless defending a family member or child, or while in defense of a premises owned or leased by the defender (dwelling or workplace). §11.81.335(b). |
| Arizona | No. Not when threatened by a forcible felony or when threatened with death, serious physical injury, or forceful removal from a residence or vehicle. §13-411(b). |
| Arkansas | Yes. A person may not use deadly force in self-defense if he or she knows that he or she can avoid the necessity of using deadly force with complete safety by retreating (§5-2-607(b)). However, NO duty to retreat exists inside a home or curtilage (§5-2-607(b)(1)(A)(b)). |
| California | No. No duty to retreat exists inside or outside the home. You are entitled to stand your ground and defend yourself and, if reasonably necessary, to pursue an assailant until the danger of bodily injury has passed. CALCRIM 3470. |
| Colorado | No. No duty to retreat exists inside or outside a dwelling, unless you are the initial aggressor in a combat situation. CRS §18-1-704(3)(b). |

| State | Duty to Retreat |
|---|---|
| Connecticut | Yes. A person is not justified in using deadly force if he or she knows that he or she can avoid the necessity of using such force with complete safety. However, no duty to retreat exists inside a dwelling or workplace. §53A-19(b). |
| Delaware | Yes, unless in a dwelling or place of work. The use of deadly force is not justified if the defendant knows the deadly force can be avoided with complete safety by retreating. §11 DEL.C.§464(e)(2). |
| Florida | No. No duty to retreat exists inside or outside a dwelling when confronted by an imminent threat of serious bodily injury or death, or to prevent the commission of a forcible felony. §776.012 |
| Georgia | No. No duty to retreat exists inside or outside a dwelling and you have the right to stand your ground in self-defense. §16-3-23.1 |
| Hawaii | No. A person employing protective force may estimate the necessity thereof under the circumstances as he believes them to be when the force is used without retreating, surrendering possession, doing any other act which he has no legal duty to do, or abstaining from any lawful action.§703-304(5)(b). No duty to retreat exists in a dwelling or place of work. §703-304(b)(1) |
| Idaho | No. No duty to retreat exists inside or outside a dwelling in the exercise of self-defense. A person may also pursue an attacker until he or the third party (being protected) has been secured from danger. ICJI 1519. |
| Illinois | Probably not. Although no statute on point exists, the common law in Illinois suggests no duty to retreat exists inside or outside a dwelling if the actor is legally in a place and does not contribute to the threat. People v. Manley |
| Indiana | No. A person does not have a duty to retreat inside or outside a dwelling if the person reasonably believes that the force is necessary to prevent serious bodily injury or the commission of a forcible felony. §35-41-3-2(a)(2). |
| Iowa | Yes. An actor must make reasonable efforts to retreat if he can do so in complete safety. However, there is no duty to retreat in a dwelling or workplace. §704.1 |

| State | Duty to Retreat |
|---|---|
| Kansas | No. An actor has no duty to retreat and has the right to stand his ground and meet force with force. An actor also has no duty to retreat in a dwelling, place of work, or vehicle. §21-3218. |
| Kentucky | No. A person does not have a duty to retreat prior to the use of deadly physical force. Likewise, no duty to retreat exists in a dwelling or vehicle. §503.050(4). |
| Louisiana | No. A person shall have no duty to retreat before using force or violence and may stand his or her ground and meet force with force. There is also no duty to retreat in a dwelling, business, or occupied vehicle. §14:19(c). |
| Maine | Yes. A person must make reasonable attempts to retreat from an encounter if he can do so in complete safety. No duty to retreat exists inside a dwelling if the person is not the initial aggressor. §17 AMRSA 108(3)(a) |
| Maryland | Yes. No statutory reference exists, however the common law appears to support the MPC's minority opinion that a duty to retreat from an encounter must be made prior to using deadly force, if it can be done in complete safety. See MPC §3.04(2)(b) |
| Massachusetts | Yes. No statutory reference exists, however the common law appears to support the MPC's minority opinion that a duty to retreat from an encounter exists prior to using deadly force, if it can be done in complete safety. See MPC §3.04(2)(b) |
| Michigan | No. An actor may use justified self-defense against another individual anywhere he or she has the legal right to be with no duty to retreat. §780.972 |
| Minnesota | Yes. No statutory reference exists, however the common law appears to support the MPC's minority opinion that a duty to retreat from an encounter exists prior to using deadly force, if it can be done in complete safety. No such duty exists inside the home. See MPC §3.04(2)(b) |
| Mississippi | No. A person shall have no duty to retreat before using deadly force to defend him or herself from an unlawful threat, so long as the person acting in self-defense is not culpable for instigating or escalating the threat. §97-3-15(4). |
| Missouri | No. SB 656 (2016) |

| State | Duty to Retreat |
|---|---|
| Montana | No. A person who is lawfully in a place and who is threatened with bodily injury or loss of life has no duty to retreat from a threat or summon law enforcement assistance prior to using force. MCA§ 4-3-110. |
| Nebraska | Yes. An actor who knows that he can avoid the necessity of using deadly force with complete safety by retreating or surrendering possession of a thing must do so. No such duty exists inside the home or workplace. §28-1409(4)(b). |
| Nevada | No. Although there is no statute on point, it appears that the common law of Nevada follows the circuit majority view that there is no duty to retreat from unlawful force both inside and outside one's habitation. See Runion v. State. |
| New Hampshire | No. A person is not justified in using deadly force on another to defend himself or herself or a third person from deadly force by the other if he or she knows that he or she and the third person can, with complete safety: <br> (a) Retreat from the encounter, except that he or she is not required to retreat if he or she is within his or her dwelling, its curtilage, or anywhere he or she has a right to be, and was not the initial aggressor; or <br> (b) Surrender property to a person asserting a claim of right thereto; or <br> (c) Comply with a demand that he or she abstain from performing an act which he or she is not obliged to perform; nor is the use of deadly force justifiable when, with the purpose of causing death or serious bodily harm, the person has provoked the use of force against himself or herself in the same encounter; or <br> (d) If he or she is a law enforcement officer or a private person assisting the officer at the officer's direction and was acting pursuant to RSA 627:5, the person need not retreat. <br> N.H. Rev. Stat. Ann. § 627:4 |
| New Jersey | Yes. The actor (has a duty to retreat) if he knows that he can avoid the necessity of using deadly force with complete safety by retreating or by surrendering possession of a thing to a person asserting a claim of right thereto, or by complying with a demand that he abstain from any action which he has no duty to take. § 2C:3-4. |

| State | Duty to Retreat |
|---|---|
| New York | Yes. A person may not use deadly physical force upon another person if…he or she knows that with complete personal safety, to oneself and others he or she may avoid the necessity of so doing by retreating, except that the actor is under no duty to retreat in his or her dwelling. §35.15(2)(a). |
| New Mexico | No. A person who is threatened with an attack need not retreat. In the exercise of his right of self-defense, he may stand his ground and defend himself. UJI §14-5190. |
| North Carolina | A person does not have a duty to retreat in any place he or she has the lawful right to be. NC ST §14-51.3 |
| North Dakota | Yes. The use of deadly force is not justified if it can be avoided, with safety to the actor and others, by retreat or other conduct involving minimal interference with the freedom of the individual menaced. There is no duty to retreat within a dwelling. §12.1-05-07 |
| Ohio | Yes. No statutory reference exists, however the common law appears to support the MPC's minority opinion that a duty to retreat from an encounter exists prior to using deadly force, if it can be done in complete safety. No such duty exists inside the home or a vehicle (§2901.09). See MPC §3.04(2)(b) |
| Oklahoma | No. A person who was not the aggressor or did not provoke another with intent to cause an altercation or did not voluntarily enter into mutual combat has no duty to retreat, but may stand firm and use the right of self-defense. OUJI-CR 8-52. |
| Oregon | No. There is no duty to retreat from an unlawful threat in Oregon, either inside or outside of a habitation. §ORS 161.219, State v. Sandoval |
| Pennsylvania | NO. A person has NO duty to retreat if: 1.The actor has the right to be in the place where he is attacked, 2.The actor believes it is immediately necessary to do so to protect himself against death, serious bodily injury, kidnapping, or sexual intercourse by force or threat; AND, 3.The person against whom the force is used displays or otherwise uses: 1.A firearm or replica firearm, or 2.Any other weapon readily or apparently capable of lethal use. 18 PACSA §505 |

| State | Duty to Retreat |
|---|---|
| Rhode Island | Yes. No statutory reference exists, however the common law appears to support the MPC's minority opinion that a duty to retreat from an encounter exists prior to using deadly force, if it can be done in complete safety. No such duty exists inside the home. See MPC §3.04(2)(b). |
| South Carolina | NO. A person who is not engaged in an unlawful activity and who is attacked in another place where he has a right to be, including, but not limited to, his place of business, has no duty to retreat and has the right to stand his ground and meet force with force, including deadly force, if he reasonably believes it is necessary to prevent death or great bodily injury to himself or another person or to prevent the commission of a violent crime as defined in Section 16-1-60. S.C. Code Ann. § 16-11-440 |
| South Dakota | No. A person does not have a duty to retreat if the person is in a place where he or she has a right to be. SDCL §22-18-4. Likewise no duty exists inside a home. |
| Tennessee | No. A person who is not engaged in unlawful activity and is in a place where such person has a right to be has no duty to retreat before threatening or using force against another person when and to the degree the person reasonably believes the force is immediately necessary to protect against another's use or attempted use of unlawful force. §39-11-611(b)(2). |
| Texas | No. A person who has a right to be present at the location where the force is used, who has not provoked the person against whom the force is used, and who is not engaged in criminal activity at the time the force is used is not required to retreat before using force. §9.31(e). There is likewise no duty to retreat inside a home, vehicle, or place of business. |
| Utah | No. A person does not have a duty to retreat from force or threatened force if the person is in a place where he has lawfully entered or remained. §76-2-402(3). There is likewise no duty to retreat inside a habitation. |
| Vermont | Yes. No statutory reference exists, however the common law appears to support the MPC's minority opinion that a duty to retreat from an encounter exists prior to using deadly force, if it can be done in complete safety. No such duty exists inside the home. See MPC §3.04(2)(b) |

| State | Duty to Retreat |
|---|---|
| Virginia | Although there are no statutes on point, it appears that the Virginia common law follows the circuit majority opinion that there is no duty to retreat either inside or outside a dwelling so long as the actor is free from fault. |
| Washington | No. Although there is no statute on point, the Washington common law supports the circuit majority opinion that there is no duty to retreat from an unlawful threat so long as the actor is free from contributory guilt. State v. Prado. |
| West Virginia | No. Although no statute exists on point, it appears the West Virginia common law supports the circuit majority opinion that no duty to retreat exists. |
| Wisconsin | Maybe outside a home, NO inside a home. Outside a home: Wisconsin's case law is ambiguous and there is no statute on point: "While there is no statutory duty to retreat, whether the opportunity to retreat was available may be a consideration regarding whether the defendant reasonably believed the force used was necessary to prevent or terminate the interference." State v. Wenger, 225 Wis. 2d 495 (1999). Inside a home: The court may not consider whether the actor had an opportunity to flee or retreat before he or she used force and shall presume that the actor reasonably believed that the force was necessary to prevent imminent death or great bodily harm to himself or herself if the actor makes such a claim under sub. (1) and either of the following applies: 1. The person against whom the force was used was in the process of unlawfully and forcibly entering the actor's dwelling, motor vehicle, or place of business, the actor was present in the dwelling, motor vehicle, or place of business, and the actor knew or reasonably believed that an unlawful and forcible entry was occurring. 2. The person against whom the force was used was in the actor's dwelling, motor vehicle, or place of business after unlawfully and forcibly entering it, the actor was present in the dwelling, motor vehicle, or place of business, and the actor knew or reasonably believed that the person had unlawfully and forcibly entered the dwelling, motor vehicle, or place of business. Wis. Stat. Ann. § 939.48 (West) |

| State | Duty to Retreat |
|-------|-----------------|
| Washington DC | Yes. No statutory reference exists, however the common law appears to support the MPC's minority opinion that a duty to retreat from an encounter exists prior to using deadly force, if it can be done in complete safety. No such duty exists inside the home. Specifically, District of Columbia courts have ruled that "reasonable steps" must be taken prior to the use of deadly force. See MPC §3.04(2)(b), Bedney v. US |
| Wyoming | Yes. No statutory reference exists, however the common law appears to support the MPC's minority opinion that a duty to retreat from an encounter exists prior to using deadly force, if it can be done in complete safety. No such duty exists inside the home. See MPC §3.04(2)(b), Baier v. State. |

# Second Amendment Articles Written By The Author

What follows are a few select articles written for national publications by the author, Phillip Nelsen, regarding foundational Second Amendment topics.

## Article 1: The Constitution Does Not Care How Much Harm Guns Cause... And That Is A Good Thing.

### _Synopsis:_
How much harm guns cause cannot serve to restrict the right to keep & bear arms. Constitutional rights are not analyzed on a risk/utility basis. From a legal perspective, the amount of societal harm that comes from the exercise of a constitutional right does not matter, and that is a very good thing.

**Related Gun Control Arguments**: "Guns cause too much harm, people have a right to feel safe. Your right to carry a gun isn't worth all the harm it causes. We need to institute [insert gun-control measure being advocated, such as more background checks, training, fees, etc.] to prevent these bad things from happening."

### Argument in Support of Synopsis:
The right to keep (which is own) a firearm is a fundamental constitutional right under the US Constitution. Further, the right to bear (which is carry) a firearm is a fundamental constitutional right under the state constitutions of dozens of states. A "fundamental right" is a right, generally found in the Bill of Rights, that is "fundamental to _our_ scheme of ordered liberty,"[1] or "deeply rooted in this Nation's history and tradition."[2] Other fundamental rights include the right to due process, right to freedom of speech, freedom of religion, right to privacy, right to marry (and procreate), right to interstate travel, etc. All fundamental rights are equal in the law, no single right takes priority over another.

The United States Supreme Court has ruled that the types of weapons Americans have a fundamental right to own are "all instruments that constitute bearable arms, even those that were not in existence at the time of the founding."[3] The argument that certain firearms should not be protected because the founders didn't envision them at the time the constitution was written will be the subject of a future article, but suffice it to say that argument is severely flawed. The US Supreme Court has responded to that argument as follows:

> "Some have made the argument, bordering on the frivolous, that only those arms in existence in the 18th century are protected by the Second Amendment. We do not interpret constitutional rights that way. Just as the First Amendment protects modern forms of communications, and the Fourth Amendment applies to modern forms of search, the Second Amendment extends, to all instruments that constitute bearable arms, even those that were not in existence at the time of the founding."[4]

A common theme amongst those seeking further gun-control is to point to the amount of harm that results from a particular incident involving firearms (such as a mass shooting) and use that harm as evidence that gun-rights need to be further regulated. However, the US Supreme Court has squarely addressed this argument, and emphatically rejected it:

> "[Gun control advocates] maintain that the Second Amendment differs from all of the other provisions of the Bill of Rights because it concerns the right to possess a deadly implement and thus has implications for public safety. And they note that there is intense disagreement on the question whether the private possession of guns in the home increases or decreases gun deaths and injuries. The right to keep and bear arms, however, is not the only constitutional right that has controversial public safety implications. All of the constitutional provisions that impose restrictions on law enforcement and on the prosecution of crimes fall into the same category. [Gun control advocates] cite no case in which we have refrained from holding that a provision of the Bill of Rights is binding on the States on the ground that the right at issue has disputed public safety implications."[5].

If we are going to limit constitutional rights based on the potential societal harm they may cause, then logic dictates we should prioritize them in order of harm. Consider for a moment if the same justification put forth in favor of gun control (that the right must be restrained until harm is ameliorated) were to be applied equally among all fundamental constitutional rights. Consider the harm caused by the below constitutionally protected rights. Read them. Think about the comparisons. Then ask yourself if you truly feel constitutional rights should be judged the way you are proposing.

**Use of The Internet**: The use of the Internet is broadly protected under the First Amendment to the US Constitution. There are an estimated 1.5-million cyber crimes committed each year in America, costing Americans a staggering annual total of over $18,000,000,000 in credit card fraud alone.[6] Tens of thousands of child sex crimes, and the distribution of millions of images of child pornography, occur online each year in this country. When discussing the harm the internet causes, the US Department of Justice said the following, "[t]he expansion of the Internet and advanced digital technology lies parallel to the explosion of the child pornography market. Child pornography images are readily available through virtually every Internet technology, including social networking websites, file-sharing sites, photo-sharing sites, gaming devices, and even mobile apps." [7] Ask yourself what you use the internet to accomplish each day (checking social media, checking bank account balances, sending emails), and then ask yourself if your right to do those things is worth the millions of crimes, including the sexual exploitation of thousands of minors, that occur on the internet each day/month/year? Not to mention the Internet is the primary medium of communication for criminal and terrorist groups.

To put this analogy into perspective, gun owners in Illinois must complete a 16-hour training course, submit to a background check, register with the state, and pay hundreds of dollars for the right to bear arms. Shall we begin requiring similar 16-hour Internet safety courses, costing hundreds of dollars, criminal background checks and require registration of individuals who are using the Internet? Shall we institute "internet free times/zones" in places where Internet crimes are most likely to occur (for example, after 10pm, or inside of bedrooms), making it prohibited by law to go online in those areas/times? You may respond, *"of course not, I am not engaged in illegal conduct on the internet so why would my rights be restricted because of the actions of a malfeasant minority of internet users?"* If you responded that way you would be correct in your logic...and now you are beginning to understand the perspective of gun owners.

To draw another internet analogy. One may ask why you *need* high-speed internet? It can logically be assumed a 56k (or even 19.2k) modem would provide normal civilians with sufficient internet access to accomplish their daily tasks. Higher speed (more dangerous) internet access should be limited only to government and military applications. It is irrefutable that high-speed internet is the internet speed of choice for cyber criminals and pedophiles. Why not restrict access to these more dangerous internet speeds to people who *need* it? This is the logic used for banning high capacity magazines and other "assault" style weapons, why not use it in this context as well?


**Right to Due Process**: The US Supreme Court has continually upheld due process rights, which include the Fifth and Sixth Amendment rights to a fair and speedy trial, as well as the right to have certain evidence excluded at trial. These rights supersede any and all harm they may cause. "The exclusionary rule generates 'substantial social costs,' which sometimes include setting the guilty free and the dangerous at large."[8] During *Miranda* – the case that gave rise to the *Miranda Warning* – the court upheld the requirement that officers inform civilians of their rights even though, "[i]n some unknown number of cases ... it will return a killer, a rapist or other criminal to the streets ... to repeat his crime."[9] When I was a prosecutor I saw this first hand. Criminals are set free daily, many of which have committed, and often confessed to, serious crimes. All because a filing deadline was missed, evidence was excluded, or testimony was not properly obtained. Despite all this harm, however, due process rights persist. Shall we reevaluate them?


**Right to Privacy**: The right to be left alone, as it has been called, is one of the most universally accepted rights we have. The people have the right "to be secure in their persons, houses, papers, and effects, against unreasonable searches and seizures." The government cannot enter your home without a warrant, monitor your activities, and so on without a warrant. The government can't even prosecute you for crimes, including murder, they can clearly prove you committed in your home if they obtain the evidence in contravention to your Fourth Amendment rights. Consider, however, the amount of bad things that happen behind closed doors in America. Domestic violence, sexual abuse, child abuse, neglect, drugs, murder. The vast majority of these crimes do not occur in public, they occur in private. Why then, using the gun control logic, do we not institute 24 hour monitoring of private places? Imagine a government issued Amazon Alexa style speaker that monitors your daily conversations, alerts when signs of abuse or illegal activities are heard, and then summons the police to come to your home. Is your right to privacy in your home more important than the millions of serious crimes that occur in homes each year? Yes, of course it is, but if you are allowing yourself to actually think about this analogy you are now better understanding the flaws in the logic used to restrict firearms.

**The Right to Marry/Procreate**: Finally, for the last example, I will mention the most dangerous and harmful right Americans have, the right to make and raise children. Although not explicitly contained anywhere in the constitution, the right to marry and have children is accepted as one of the most fundamental rights we have (with the right to marry being specifically ruled on recently by the Supreme Court). You do not need a permit to make babies. You do not need to demonstrate you are a responsible and capable parent to make babies. There is no limit on the number of babies you can make. There are no laws requiring you to be sober when making babies. There are no tests, trainings, or other qualifications to be eligible to make babies. There are also no restrictions on what you can teach your babies. I could conceivably make 150 children, teach them all to be terrible, violent, racist, sexist and otherwise awful people, and as long as I keep them moderately fed and clothed, the government will not take them from me. Consider, however, the amount of societal harm that comes from bad parents and irresponsible procreation. I will proffer that there is no act that results in more harm to society than irresponsible procreation. However, despite all of that, there are relatively no restrictions on this activity. Two drug addicted 12-year olds can make babies in this country. Why? Why do we not mandate required parenting classes, drug tests, financial disclosures, procreation permits, home inspections, etc.? Why don't we put people in jail who make babies without having the proper permits, training, insurance and government issued license? Adoption requires many of these things, but procreation requires none. Why? The reason should be obvious by now. Even though the right to procreate has infinite potential societal harm, it is a fundamental right nonetheless and is not subject to indiscriminate restriction simply because of the potential harm it may cause.

Those still not convinced by this logic will rebut by saying something along the lines of, *"but when was the last time any of those rights resulted in [insert number] of children being killed?"* That question, of course, is short sighted and ignores the fact that restricting any number of constitutional rights could prevent mass shootings. If we disregard due process and the First Amendment we could put people in jail the moment they post a threat on the Internet (the way the recent Florida shooter did), thus preventing many of these tragedies. If government cameras monitored inside a shooter's home, maybe they would have caught them plotting. If a warrant wasn't required police officers could simply enter someone's home and search their home/computer any time they receive a tip that someone might be dangerous (like the FBI received a tip for the Florida shooter).

The reality is those seeking more gun control aren't bad people, and they aren't unintelligent. However, as demonstrated by this article, this logic being used to promote further restrictions on the fundamental right to keep and bear arms is flawed. It cannot be accepted or promulgated.

Gun control advocates want to protect children. Pro-gun advocates likewise want to protect children. Let us put aside our cognitive bias and look at things as they truly are. People are all dramatically different and similar at the same time. Psychologists have soundly demonstrated human beings can look at the same thing, and see very different things, often even missing something that should be completely obvious to anyone. Einstein, while pondering why people think the way they do, noted that people find difficulty understanding simple concepts "when an experience comes into conflict with a world of concepts already sufficiently fixed within us." [10] It is time to put aside that *world of concepts* and accept truth for what it is.

I am not making an argument, in this article, that guns make America safer (that argument will be set forth in the next article). Instead, **I am simply stating that it does not matter if guns make us more safe, or less safe, in the eyes of the Constitution.** Of course it matters from a perspective of compassion, humanity and emotion, but Constitutional rights are not evaluated subjectively and do not care about the compassion or emotion of those who exercise them. They exist independent of the harm they cause and they persist in their course even if they harm us all. That is the nature of fundamental rights, and until we all understand that simple principle, we cannot have any degree of productive discourse.

Sources:

[1] *Duncan,* 391 U.S., at 149, 88 S.Ct. 1444

[2] McDonald v. City of Chicago, Ill., 561 U.S. 742, 767, 130 S. Ct. 3020, 3036, 177 L. Ed. 2d 894 (2010)

[3] D.C. v. Heller, 554 U.S. 570, 582, 128 S. Ct. 2783, 2791–92, 171 L. Ed. 2d 637 (2008)

[4] D.C. v. Heller, 554 U.S. 570, 582, 128 S. Ct. 2783, 2791–92, 171 L. Ed. 2d 637 (2008)

[5] *Id.*

[6] http://www.cbs.com/shows/csi-cyber/news/1003888/these-cybercrime-statistics-will-make-you-think-twice-about-your-password-where-s-the-csi-cyber-team-when-you-need-them-/

[7] https://www.justice.gov/criminal-ceos/child-pornography

[8] *Barker v. Wingo,* 407 U.S. 514, 522, 92 S.Ct. 2182, 33 L.Ed.2d 101 (1972)

[9] *Miranda v. Arizona,* 384 U.S. 436, 517, 86 S.Ct. 1602, 16 L.Ed.2d 694 (1966)

[10] http://www.worldcat.org/title/autobiographical-notes/oclc/4940678&referer=brief_results

# Article 2: A Pragmatic Argument In Favor Of Letting Teachers Be Armed

**Preface**: This article is intended to make a logic driven argument, supported by evidence and reason, that teachers, faculty and administrators should be allowed to take individual accountability for their safety, and the safety of those in their classrooms. The reality is, short of dispatching with evil there is no *good* solution to this problem. There are two terms often used when discussing mass shootings, *"stop"* and *"prevent"*. Those terms are not synonymous in this context. *Prevention* of mass shootings is a social science discussion that involves a potentially infinite number of variables. I am not qualified to speak on that topic, therefore I won't. *Stopping* mass shootings, however, entails a discussion of how to quickly and decisively end a violent attack on our schools, a much more reactive analysis. In that regard I am qualified to speak, and that is the only topic discussed in this article. I am a college professor. I am a parent of small children who I drop off at school daily. I have hundreds of other people's children in my college classes each semester. I care a great deal about my students. I understand this issue, much more than most. I take it seriously. I am also a firearm instructor and armed security guard instructor, who has spent the last decade running one of the largest civilian firearm training companies in America, instructing over 150,000 people in nearly 30 states in our training courses.

I understand many others, roughly half of our country, feel differently than I do about this issue, and have different backgrounds than I do. Cognitive bias and confirmation bias are real. We all want to hear viewpoints that agree with us, and that includes me. Einstein, while pondering why people think the way they do, noted that people find difficulty understanding new concepts *"when an experience comes into conflict with a world of concepts already sufficiently fixed within us."*[1] My hope in this article is to address this issue, which affects us all, in a way that invokes a pensive discussion and sparks a desire to look outside the status quo *world of concepts*. I am not writing this for people who agree with me, I am writing it for those who don't. I will not use intentionally inflammatory language, nor will I make reference to any political parties or cast mass judgments. Our society is beginning to view screaming at someone with differing views, in an attempt to silence them, as acceptable discourse. It is not. We must be better than that. Please consider what I have written below, and respond with your thoughts. I will welcome hearing differing, civil, views.

**Synopsis: Training A Relatively Small Percentage Of Teachers To Obtain A Variety Of Skills, Including First-Aid, Tactical Firearm Skills, And Threat Assessment, In The Same Manner Armed Security, Law Enforcement And Airline Pilots Are Currently Trained, Would Be A Cost Effective And Practical Step To Curb Mass Shootings In American Schools.**

*Related Gun Control Argument:* Guns have no place in education. Our students shouldn't have to worry about guns while learning. A teacher is more likely to harm a student than stop a bad guy. Teachers aren't capable of stopping bad guys. More guns won't solve this problem.

## Argument in Support of Synopsis:

The right to self-preservation, that is the right to defend oneself from violent attack, is the most fundamental right any human being has.[2] In comparison to the right to self-preservation, all other rights must logically be placed in subordination. After all, if your life may be taken from you then what good is a right to vote, or a right to speak, or a right to marry? As with all fundamental rights, the right to self-preservation is also an individual right. The individual right status means, just as I cannot be compelled to forfeit my right to vote to the government to vote in my stead, or my right to speak to the government to speak in my stead, I should not be compelled to outsource my individual right to personal protection to the government. I can, of course, voluntarily choose to forfeit any of my rights, but I should not be compelled to do so. Like all rights, however, my right to self-preservation is not limitless. There are reasonable, limited, restraints placed on all constitutional rights. The oft cited *yelling fire in a theater*, for example, is not protected by the First Amendment. My wife and I have the right to procreate without the government interfering, but I can't do it on a public sidewalk. Knowing this, educators (like myself) should be entitled to one of two things.

Either:

1.  Our schools should be secured in a manner reasonably calculated to ensure no one with a firearm/weapon may enter (like our airports); or

2.  A system should be established to enable faculty, staff and administrators who possess the proper certifications and training to carry firearms at their place of employment.

Anything less than the above is a violation of the fundamental rights of those who work in education. You cannot strip millions of Americans of their right to defend themselves, and provide no alternative to ensure their safety. Such a course is illogical. Such a course violates the most basic of civil rights. Such a course is destined to see a continuation of the destruction we are currently seeing.

The Cost & Practicality of Security Screening:

Security screenings, like those in post 9-11 airports are staggeringly expensive. Costing roughly 8 billion dollars annually[3], and failing to detect threats roughly 95% of the time[4], one can question the viability or efficacy of rolling out a similar program for our schools. With nearly twenty times more public schools in America than airports[5], and with education spending a constant political issue, we can assume an expenditure of $160 billion to install airport style security in our schools is not something we will see. Simple magnetometers and lock down protocols, such as those commonly used by courthouses and sports arenas are a much more cost-effective alternative. However, given the nature of most school campuses (including colleges) where students are routinely leaving buildings and reentering buildings in a rush to get to their next class, the practicality of a metal detector search across all schools is dubious. It could certainly be installed in many schools, likely with great deterrent effect, but it is not a practical solution across the board (including at the institution where I teach).

### The Cost & Practicality of Allowing Armed Educators:

The Washington Post analyzed the cost of training and arming educators, estimating the cost of doing so with 20% of our educators (or 718,000 individuals) at between $718 million to $1 billion.[6] That number assumes that there would not be a centralized training system for all educators, at a central location, like we have for our airline pilots (discussed more below). It also assumes that all of these educators would need to be trained from a starting point of zero, something that is unlikely and also discussed below. However, assuming the cost estimates are true, as outlined below, training and arming educators is still a significantly cheaper and more practical option to stop (not necessarily prevent) school shootings than airport style security screening.

## The Numbers:

In 2018 there are 3,160,000 public school teachers in primary and secondary schools, and 1.5 million college professors, resulting in an estimated 4.7 million educators at public institutions.[7] This number does not include any support staff, administration and other employees of these institutions, which would likely triple or quadruple that number. One can logically assume that educator pool of 4.7 million is comprised of a very diverse group of individuals, with a wide array of backgrounds and skills. One thing all of them have in common, however, is a disproportionally clean criminal background.[8] It is impossible to accurately estimate how many of these individuals would be of the nature qualified, and willing, to carry a firearm safely and efficiently. We can assume many of those with past military and law enforcement experience would have sufficiently demonstrated that capability. The number of former military and law enforcement working in education is not tracked, but it is safe to assume a not-insignificant number of them work in education (some studies show a fourfold increase in vets working in education in recent years).[9] In addition to military and law enforcement, of course, you also have a large demographic of educators who possess significant skills and training in firearms, but have never been in the military or law enforcement. I, for example, have been a firearm instructor for over a decade, and an armed security guard instructor, and have either taught or been a student in well over 3,000 hours of formal firearm training courses. To put that into perspective, it takes roughly 700 hours of training to become a police officer.[10] I have had hundreds of current and former police officers come to my courses to further their training (which is admirable and humbling). I do not classify myself as a tactical expert, and certainly not a "gun fighter", but my training and sound skill set with a firearm is not something that can be easily disregarded. None of the other college professors in my department know of my background, and my situation can be logically extended to a large number of other individuals working in education. Given that, it is difficult to estimate the total number of educators who might possess the skills and training necessary to act as sentries at our schools. To assume there are not a significant number of them, however, is irrational.

## The Airline Pilot Analogy:

NBC News recently published a piece on President Trump's proposal to arm teachers. The report was entirely devoid of contrasting opinions, and featured the following commentary by Dr. David Hemenway, a professor of health policy at Harvard School of Public Health:

*"It's a crazy proposal." Chuckling, he added, "So what should we do about reducing airline hijacking? Give all the passengers guns as they walk on?"*

What the blissfully amused Dr. Hemenway fails to identify, however, is that we did almost that exact thing after 9-11, and we haven't had a hijacking since. No, we didn't "give all the passengers guns", instead we instituted a volunteer training program for our pilots and created a pathway for them to carry firearms on planes so long as they demonstrated sufficient skill and safety, as well as passed the amplified background checks.

Throughout most of American history Airline pilots have always been allowed to carry firearms on planes, except for a brief period between 1988-2002, during which time security of airports became more centralized and firearm regulations on planes more rigorous and, related or not to this policy, the 9-11 attack occurred. In 2002, in response to 9-11, Congress reauthorized (formally this time) pilots to carry firearms and allocated up to 900 million to train up to 85,000 volunteer airline pilots at a facility in Artesia, New Mexico (roughly $10,500 per pilot).[11] To date, roughly 13,800 pilots are estimated to have completed the six-day training and are currently carrying firearms. That is roughly 10% of the overall pilot population. It is notable that airline pilots are required to travel to the training at their own cost, and take the time off work without pay (foregoing upwards of $2,000 in pay).[12] This willingness to make this sacrifice represents an unanticipated desire by pilots to provide for their own safety, as well as that of the passengers.

It is not difficult, even for the most biased mind, to draw an analogy between our teachers and our pilots. Both are put in charge of groups of people (ranging in number from 30-200) for a number of hours each day. Both are subject to pre-hire background checks and must demonstrate a sound psychological mindset. Both are charged with dealing with unruly individuals in their sphere, and both are given broad discretion on how to deal with high stress situations. Pilots are the metaphorical teachers of the sky. No, it is not an exact analogy, but it is not far off. By all accounts the armed airline pilot program has been a success. No, a pilot has not had to use their weapon to stop a hijacker yet, but that is precisely the point. Avoiding and deterring a violent attack is the best way to defeat an attacker. Knowing this, why could the process used to train airline pilots not be adapted, expanded, and rolled out to our educators? It has certainly worked flawlessly in Utah schools.

**The Utah Case Study:**

Many engaged in this debate would be surprised to learn that we have at least 16 years (and as many as 26 years) of empirical data we can study to find out what would happen if educators were allowed to possess guns in schools. During its 2004 General Session, the Utah Legislature passed Utah Code section 63−98−102, a statute prohibiting state and local entities from enacting or enforcing any ordinance, regulation, rule, or policy that in "any way inhibits or restricts the possession or use of firearms on either public or private property."[13] This law change explicitly prohibited public schools from preventing anyone with a Utah concealed firearm permit from carrying a firearm, in any manner, onto any public school property (kindergarten through college). Since that time thousands of educators, staff and even legal-age college students have carried their firearms onto Utah schools daily. At least 253,404 people in Utah have concealed firearm permits (or roughly 11% of the adult population).[14] There are 175,000 college students in Utah, and another 60,000 college faculty and staff, resulting in roughly 235,000 adults on Utah public college campuses each day.[15] Carrying those numbers forward, and recognizing this is not an exact calculation, it is logical to assume as many as 23,000 people on Utah college campuses are licensed to carry firearms every day. That is not an insignificant number, and it says nothing for the number of faculty and staff carrying in Utah elementary and secondary schools. Despite that very high number, and knowing this has been the case for at least 14 years, Utah college campuses have seen zero shootings in that time period. Wow! How can this possibly be ignored? In a national debate where this exact topic is being discussed, how can anyone with intellectual integrity disregard 14 years of empirical data on the exact subject they are debating? If cognitive bias were a band of gorillas, ignoring this is King Kong beating his chest on top of the Empire State Building.

The doomsday projections of what would happen if we allowed educators (and even college students) to carry firearms must, if they are to be intellectually honest, acknowledge that they have come to fruition **not once** in Utah during the past 14 years of real-world experimentation. Like Utah, several other states including Colorado (and more recently Texas) have seen similar non-doomsday results of allowing firearms on school campuses.

That's not to say Utah has not had a mass shooting, it's just the shooter selected a small mall, and not a school, for his target. The reason *why* the shooter made this decision, however, is worth discussing. On February 12, 2007, a lone terrorist entered Trolley Square Mall with a pump action shotgun and a .38 special revolver (two firearms that do not fit the traditional gun-control narrative). After killing five victims the shooter was engaged by an off-duty police officer in plain clothes named Ken Hammond. Ken exchanged gunfire with the shooter, not striking him, but drawing his attention away to give others the chance to retreat. The total duration of the shooting lasted 6 minutes. It is key to this discussion, however, to note that the University of Utah is less than 3 miles from Trolley Square Mall. I was one of the 32,000 students attending the University of Utah that day, it was a Monday. Trolley Square Mall is a very small mall, comparative to other malls in Salt Lake. Why would the shooter not have chosen the University of Utah campus or the much larger Gateway Mall for his target? We will never know his true motive, but it is worth noting that unlike the University of Utah and the larger malls in the area, Trolley Square Mall had a large sign posted at each entrance prohibiting firearms on the property (click here to see the sign). A news broadcast that night featured a witness who stated something to the effect, "*I saw the shooter. I looked for something to throw at him, but all I could find was a stool.*" It could very well be mere chance that the shooter happened to choose the one high traffic location in Salt Lake City where firearms were overtly prohibited without any security, but it could also be very much correlated.

**Call to Action**: The following steps should be implemented immediately:

1. Perform a professional security assessment of American schools. Determine which schools would be good candidates for magnetometer searches and security screenings.

2. Establish magnetometers and security screenings at schools where the logistics of the buildings allow doing so.

3. Immediately establish a robust training and mental health screening process to certify educators and staff to carry firearms on school campuses where magnetometers are not an option, in a similar way airline pilots are currently trained.

4. Implement any and all other reasonably calculated societal changes needed to curb the mental health crises and make our children safer, so long as those changes respect the inalienable fundamental rights of the citizens.

**Conclusion**: Based on the foregoing, allowing a small demographic of trained and voluntary participants to carry firearms during the regular course of employment is the most cost-effective and practical solution to respond to an active school shooting.

**Sources:**

[1]  http://www.worldcat.org/title/autobiographical-notes/oclc/4940678&referer=brief_results

[2] D.C. v. Heller, 554 U.S. 570, 582, 128 S. Ct. 2783, 2791–92, 171 L. Ed. 2d 637 (2008)

[3] https://politicalscience.osu.edu/faculty/jmucller/JATMfin.pdf

[4]  http://abcnews.go.com/US/tsa-director-reassigned-wake-security-failures/story?id=31458476

[5] https://nces.ed.gov/fastfacts/display.asp?id=84

[6]  https://www.washingtonpost.com/news/politics/wp/2018/02/22/the-economics-of-arming-americas-schools/?utm_term=.796b027fb8c7

[7]  https://www.statista.com/statistics/185012/number-of-teachers-in-elementary-and-secondary-schools-since-1955/

[8]  https://www.usatoday.com/story/news/2016/02/14/how-we-graded-states-teacher-background-checks/80214540/

[9]  https://www.usatoday.com/story/news/nation/2013/01/02/soldier-teachers/1804537/

[10] https://www.cnn.com/2016/09/28/us/jobs-training-police-trnd/index.html

[11] https://www.washingtonpost.com/archive/politics/2007/02/25/more-airline-pilots-training-to-carry-a-gun-and-badge/521c4ebf-22d7-48a7-84d7-e73a98bb865a/?utm_term=.8d6d6c0cf834

[12]  https://www.washingtontimes.com/news/2015/aug/2/tracy-price-arm-pilots-to-restoring-safety-in-airl/

[13] Univ. of Utah v. Shurtleff, 2006 UT 51, ¶ 1, 144 P.3d 1109, 1111

[14] https://bci.utah.gov/wp-content/uploads/sites/15/2018/01/2017Q4.pdf

[15]  https://higheredutah.org/enrollment-at-utahs-public-colleges-universities-increases-by-over-4000/

# Article 3: On Interacting With Law Enforcement

***DISCLAIMER TO OUR LEO FRIENDS**: This article is not meant to offend or insult anyone in law enforcement. It is meant to apprise the readers of their constitutional rights. Like all law enforcement, while in uniform you are an actor of the state. However, when you take off the uniform you are also a citizen fully equipped with all the same constitutional liberties as those you interact with on your job. As such, this information should be appreciated by you in your individual capacity, and hopefully respected by you when acting on behalf of the state. The readers of this article are mainly concealed firearm permit holders. Meaning, they are exceptionally law abiding citizens. It is not our intent to help criminals conceal firearms during traffic stops, we simply want to help the law abiding remain law abiding while navigating a very complicated spiderweb of firearm laws.*

Let's have a very blunt conversation about interacting with law enforcement while in possession of a firearm. This article is not meant to focus on *when* a police officer has a legal right to stop you, but instead is meant to cover the less analyzed issue of **what are the legal implications of informing an officer that you are carrying a firearm?** I am going to offer this article from a purely legal standpoint, the same way I would advise a client. There are obviously differing opinions on how you *should* handle a police stop. It is not my intent to address how you *should*, but instead to analyze what the legal implications are of certain conduct during a stop.

Let's start at the beginning. Relating to police stops of concealed permit holders there are three categories of states, namely:

∞ **Duty to Inform States**: States where you are required by law to affirmatively disclose the presence of your firearm (e.g. Ohio, Michigan, etc.).

∞ **Quasi Duty to Inform States:** IIn addition to the above Duty to Inform states, some states have quasi duty to inform laws. These laws require that a permit holder must have his/her permit in their possession and surrender it upon the request of an officer. The specific requirements of these laws will vary from state to state. It is important to note that being required to give an officer your permit once it is asked of you (quasi duty to inform), and being required to affirmatively tell an officer you have a firearm without being prompted (duty to inform) are two very different legal requirements. Examples of these states are Iowa and Texas.

∞ **No Duty to Inform States:** Finally, some states are No Duty To Inform states. Meaning, there are no laws that require a gun owner to affirmatively inform an officer if they have a firearm. Additionally there are also no laws that require them to respond or provide a permit if asked about the presence of a firearm. In these states the question arises as to whether one should inform an officer about the firearm or not. Our advice is...maybe. Obviously it is highly encouraged to be courteous and respectful at all times when interacting with law enforcement. However, there are several implications of informing an officer that you have a firearm that you should be aware of before making your decision.

This article is not meant to be a state by state summary of these laws. Instead, I want to walk you through what the legal implications are of disclosing the presence of your weapon to a police officer.

IMPLICATION NUMBER 1: WAIVING YOUR FOURTH AMENDMENT RIGHTS

A potential outcome of informing an officer that you have a firearm is that the officer might then have the ability to perform what is called a *Terry Stop* or a *Terry Frisk*. The *Terry Doctrine* stems from a 1968 Supreme Court case, *Terry v. Ohio*. In *Terry*, the United States Supreme Court held that an officer may perform a protective frisk and search pursuant to a lawful stop when the officer reasonably believes a person is "**armed and presently dangerous to the officer or others**." (see: 392 U.S. 1, 24, 88 S.Ct. 1868, 20 L.Ed.2d 889 (1968)). This also gives the officer authority to temporarily disarm the permit holder "in the interest of officer safety." The Court did caution that a search "is a serious intrusion upon the sanctity of the person" and should not be taken lightly. Still, the basis for the search itself is largely left up to the officer's discretion once he is made aware of the presence of a weapon.

The sole purpose for allowing the frisk/search is to protect the officer and other prospective victims by neutralizing potential weapons. (see: *Michigan v. Long*, 463 U.S. 1032, 1049 n. 14, 103 S.Ct. 3469). As an example, a Terry Stop allows a police officer to remove you from your vehicle, pat down all occupants of the vehicle (using the sense of touch to determine if they are armed), as well as search the entire passenger compartment of the vehicle including any locked containers that might reasonably house a weapon. In other words, telling a police officer you have a firearm on you or in your vehicle can serve as a waiver of your Fourth Amendment rights and allow the officer to conduct a warrantless search.

This issue was recently highlighted in a recent 4th Circuit Court of Appeals case United States v. Robinson. In Robinson, the court extended the *Terry Doctrine* further than it previously had. In its ruling, the court stated that because firearms are "categorically dangerous":

> *an officer who makes a lawful traffic stop and who has a reasonable suspicion that one of the automobile's occupants is armed may frisk that individual for the officer's protection and the safety of everyone on the scene."*

Or as Judge Wynn ominously wrote in his concurring opinion, "*those who chose to carry firearms sacrifice certain constitutional protections afforded to individuals who elect not to carry firearms."*

The waiver of your Fourth Amendment rights is why states with "duty to inform" laws create such a constitutional dilemma. If, as a condition to carrying a firearm, I am required by law to inform an officer that I have a firearm in my vehicle, then I am simultaneously required to waive my Fourth Amendment privacy rights. That is a violation of the unconstitutional-conditions doctrine and is long overdue for a legal challenge.

> *BUT PHIL, POLICE OFFICERS ONLY PUT CRIMINALS IN JAIL, AND I'M NOT A CRIMINAL!!! WHY WOULD I CARE IF I GET SEARCHED?!?*

## IMPLICATION NUMBER 2: YOU ARE A CRIMINAL, YOU JUST DON'T KNOW IT...YET

You are a criminal, we all are from time to time. Do you have any idea how many gun laws there are out there? No? Neither does our own department of justice. If you don't even know how many gun laws there are, how can you possibly know you are abiding by all of them simultaneously? Justice Robert Jackson (U.S.

Supreme Court Justice) once said, "any lawyer worth his salt will tell the suspect [his client], in no uncertain terms, to make no statement to the police, under [any] circumstances." The reasoning behind Justice Jackson's quote isn't because police officers are bad, it is simply because the average civilian has no idea how many laws they may be breaking at any given time. As a prosecutor, and later a defense attorney, I deal with clients routinely that are charged with crimes they had no idea they were committing.

Here is a simple example of how the "*I have nothing to hide*" mentality can land you in jail. Let's imagine you are a Utah resident and a Utah concealed permit holder. Your Utah permit is valid in well over 30 states, so you decide to take a road trip with your firearm. As you're driving through Idaho (where your permit is valid) you get pulled over for speeding in a school zone. Because you are an upstanding citizen and you have nothing to hide, you tell the officer that you have a firearm in the vehicle. Aaaaannd now you're a felon. Wait, what? How did that happen? Let's review why you're now a felon.

18 U.S.C.A. § 922(q)(2)(A), otherwise known as the Federal Gun-Free School Zones Act (GFSZA), states that:

> It shall be unlawful for any individual knowingly to possess a firearm that has moved in or that otherwise affects interstate or foreign commerce at a place that the individual knows, or has reasonable cause to believe, is a school zone.

The term "school zone" means in, or on the grounds of, a public, parochial or private school; or within a distance of 1,000 feet from the grounds of a public, parochial or private school. The term "school" means a school which provides elementary or secondary education, as determined under State law (see 18 U.S.C.A. § 921).

There are a few narrow exceptions to this law, one of which is:

> "if the individual possessing the firearm is licensed to do so **by the State in which the school zone is located** or a political subdivision of the State, and the law of the State or political subdivision requires that, before an individual obtains such a license, the law enforcement authorities of the State or political subdivision verify that the individual is qualified under law to receive the license;" 18 U.S.C.A. § 922 (emphasis added)

You have a permit from Utah which is valid in Idaho, but was not issued by Idaho, which means this federal law is in full force against you. See how fun that is? Don't worry, the penalty for violating the law is only 5 years in prison and a $5,000 fine. If you would like more details about this law you can read the ATF's analysis of it here.

Of course, as is often the case, the Idaho police officer may sympathize that you are not intending to violate the law and may choose not to escalate the situation beyond a mere traffic stop. Millions of people violate the GFSZA every year and few are prosecuted. Given the harsh penalty, however, it's not a gamble I personally want to take.

## IMPLICATION NUMBER 3: SEARCHES ARE ALMOST ALWAYS BAD.

I would challenge anyone reading this to think of any instance where someone waiving their rights, or consenting to a search/seizure, has made their life better. In my career I certainly haven't seen it. I have, however, seen a significant amount of good people get charged with serious crimes because they were overly generous with the amount of information they shared with law enforcement. It is my experience that nothing good can come from waiving your rights. Consider the wording of the the oft cited Miranda warning:

> *The warning of the right to remain silent must be accompanied by the explanation that anything said can and will be used **against** the individual in court. Miranda v. Arizona, 384 U.S. 436, 469, 86 S. Ct. 1602, 1625, 16 L. Ed. 2d 694 (1966) (emphasis added).*

Can and will be used *against* you. The best case scenario of waiving your rights is you get to go home. The worst case scenario is you go to prison.

Once again, it is not our intent to tell you how you should interact with law enforcement or imply in any way that law enforcement are villains or out to get you. As a prosecutor I worked with law enforcement every day, and as a firearm instructor over the past decade I can say some of the best people I know are police officers. Police officers, by and large, support the shooting sports community and are members of it themselves. We strongly encourage everyone to treat law enforcement with respect. Very little is accomplished in life by acting belligerent, rude or demeaning.

# STAY LEGAL. STAY SAFE.

## 877-252-1055

### LegalHeat.com

**GET THE APP**       **VISIT THE SITE**       **BUY THE BOOK**

# GET THE **FREE** GUN LAW APP

Visit [LegalHeat.com/app](LegalHeat.com/app) or scan the QR below to learn more about our free gun law app and download it on Android or iOS today!